Learn
MANAGEMENT SKILLS FOR LIBRARIES AND INFORMATION AGENCIES

International Edition

Bob Pymm

TotalRecall Publications, Inc..
1103 Middlecreek
Friendswood, Texas 77546
281-992-3131   281-482-5390 Fax
www.totalrecallpress.com

ISBN: 978-1-59095-437-9
UPC: 6-43977-44378-6

Printed in the United States of America with simultaneous printing in Australia, Canada, and United Kingdom.

FIRST EDITION
1 2 3 4 5 6 7 8 9 10

Library of Congress Control Number: 2015941336

TABLE OF CONTENTS

INTRODUCTION

This workbook covers the skills necessary for an entry level supervisor involved in managing a work area in a library, information center or related information environment. Its hands-on, practical approach, together with its emphasis on planning and evaluation, provides a sound framework within which a new supervisor may manage competently and effectively.

The text is a practical introduction for the novice manager or supervisor, and avoids in-depth discussion of the theoretical issues surrounding the practices discussed. It particularly focuses on skills and practices relevant to information industries. For additional management theory, you may wish to use *Learn management skills for library and information agencies* in conjunction with a more general management textbook.

Throughout the book you will find exercises to practice your skills and test your understanding. There are answers for self-checking at the back of the book. You may not always agree completely with these answers; in many cases there are no 'right' answers for problems involving perceptions and interpretation. The rationale behind each answer should provide sufficient information to enable you to understand how a particular answer was arrived at, and to show where the author took an approach different to yours.

Great emphasis has been placed on scenarios and associated readings, to illustrate useful management skills related to a particular chapter. These are directly relevant to library and information agency work, and they offer practical examples that illustrate the application of theory. They are as realistic as possible and, in most cases, they reflect actual incidents. You are strongly encouraged to take these scenarios seriously, working in small groups to evaluate the situations.

Note on Spelling and Capitalization

This edition is designed for use in North America, Europe and Australasia, across countries that employ different spelling conventions for English words. For consistency, American spelling has been adopted for the text.

Titles included in the text are capitalized according to standard library cataloging practice—that is, apart from names, only the first word of the title has a capital letter. This is intended to accustom library students and staff to this style.

Acknowledgements

Thanks to colleagues at various workplaces who, wittingly or unwittingly, provided much of the raw material for the exercises and scenarios used in the text! Also, thanks to the many students over the years who acted as guinea-pigs for much of the text and made valuable comments that helped shape the final product.

CHAPTER ONE
Managers and Their Roles

Introduction

Any task requiring the coordination of a number of elements needs to be managed. An example is building a swimming pool that requires planning to ensure that:

- it is sited properly and meets local government requirements
- the cement or fiberglass shell arrives after the hole is dug
- proper filtration is installed
- the installer arrives on schedule
- proper fencing is installed before the pool is filled with water, and so on.

It is a process that needs managing.

So too, in organizations striving to achieve complicated objectives, management skills are needed in order to ensure that things run smoothly.

 Management is the process whereby a complex task is completed satisfactorily with and through the use of other people and resources.

Management Functions

Managers have a broad responsibility to deal with resources (the people, capital, information, and technology) and the process (the procedures and practices needed to get the work done). Essentially, they organize and coordinate work activities in order to achieve goals. To do this work effectively, managers need to undertake the following related activities:

- planning
- organizing
- leading
- controlling.

Planning

Management includes planning—both short- and long-term—for the organization as a whole, for work units within the organization, and for individuals.

A manager's planning includes the clear articulation of objectives to be achieved, determining the resources required to reach these objectives, preparing budgets and timelines, and prioritizing tasks.

Long-term planning inevitably involves change of some sort; therefore consultative planning helps in the management of this change, leading to better outcomes for all concerned.

Proper planning, in consultation with staff and user groups, will help to ensure correct alignment between the priorities of the organization, the concerns of staff, and the needs of users.

Organizing

Organizing ensures that resources such as staff, equipment, appropriate training, and materials are available when needed. Resource use must be monitored and corrective action taken as appropriate. In addition, establishing procedures and work flows, preparing appropriate documentation, and monitoring work practices are all part of the organization required to put plans into effect.

Leading

Leading is needed to motivate, encourage, and enthuse staff to achieve both the organization's goals and their own. Leadership includes supporting and setting the conditions to help motivate staff, mentoring individuals, modeling appropriate behaviors, and creating the right environment for the development of individual potential.

 Without the encouragement and support of management, staff will lack motivation and involvement, with consequent costs to the organization.

Controlling

Controlling is needed to ensure that progress toward the goals proceeds as expected. Controlling requires proper procedures, milestones, and standards (again in consultation with staff expected to do the work) against which progress can be measured.

Controlling also ensures that legislation, procedures, and practices are followed; that quality standards and timeliness are monitored; and that work practices are properly documented.

Staff Expectations, Management Expectations

It is useful to consider in more depth the role of leading and supporting staff, as this is one of the more difficult and demanding tasks faced by managers at any level, and impinges directly on all other aspects of their job. It is also an area where perceptions of the task can differ radically between managers and their staff.

A good way to find out the extent to which these perceptions differ (and thus to highlight areas where conflict or misunderstanding may arise) is to ask managers what they think their leadership role entails and then to ask the same question of the staff they manage. If there is a reasonable level of agreement between the two groups, then their expectations will be similar and their objectives will be achieved more smoothly. If, on the other hand, there are quite different views, then problems may well arise that will reduce organizational effectiveness.

Management Expectations

In an informal survey undertaken in a small government agency, managers were asked to list what they wanted from their staff. The following were most commonly expected:

- deliver agreed outputs by agreed deadlines
- reach agreed quality standards

- accept personal responsibility for the outputs and deadlines
- try to improve systems and processes
- be a loyal, effective, and contributing team member
- participate in meetings and discussions
- support management decisions once consultation and discussion are completed
- share responsibility for personal development and training
- assist other team members as required
- bring concerns initially to their immediate supervisor
- implement occupational safety and health policies and practices.

Staff Expectations

In the same survey, staff were asked what they would like to see managers provide, and listed the following:

- guidance and leadership of the group
- respect for the team and individuals
- a safe, healthy, and 'respecting' work environment
- opportunities for group or individual input to decisions that affect them
- creative and innovative solutions to problems
- negotiated deadlines and priorities
- adequate resources to undertake the task
- delegation of responsibility
- adequate training and opportunities for career development
- effective representation of the area to higher management and to outside organizations or peer groups
- a good two-way information flow between upper management and the work group
- fair and proper recruitment and promotion practices
- the ability and the will to implement 'hard' decisions.

Note that there are similarities between both groups that should make it easier to work together. But in addition, there are differing views of what managers and staff expect of themselves and each other. Being aware of these differences can help overcome difficulties and assist managers to meet the challenges of their leadership role.

EXERCISE 1.1

Liz heads the circulation desk in a busy public library. She has to ensure that it runs smoothly and that it is properly staffed at all times. Including temps, there are 15 staff who do this work. Some only work weekends; some work purely at the circulation desk; and some work at the desk and do other duties such as shelve, answer reference questions, etc. The director of the library mentioned to Liz the other day that she was concerned that not enough staff were scheduled to fill the evening shift at the desk: this time appeared to be increasingly busy, now that the nearby supermarket was open late. She asked Liz to draw up a new schedule with two staff on the desk at all times, but without increasing costs or giving people shifts longer than four hours.

The main management functions are listed below. Under each heading, describe what Liz must do to accomplish this task.

Planning

Organizing

Leading

Controlling

Management Skills

In order to undertake the functions just described, managers need to develop three broad groups of skills:
- human skills
- technical skills
- conceptual skills.

Human Skills

Human skills (frequently called people skills) are essential to allow a manager to get the best out of the work team. With these skills, a manager can:
- motivate
- lead
- inspire
- build confidence
- resolve disputes
- train and develop staff
- and create an appropriate work atmosphere that values both people and productivity.

Technical Skills

Technical skills are those needed to enable a manager to understand the nature of the work being done.

Managers do not need a high level of proficiency in all the technical skills they supervise, but they must understand enough of the process to appreciate the time a task might take and the resources it requires. Without an adequate appreciation of the work and skills, a manager cannot help to resolve problems, will have difficulty setting satisfactory performance targets, and will be unsure of the standards needed for quality work.

Conceptual Skills

Conceptual skills are important for understanding the 'big picture', thinking long-term, and understanding the consequences of actions. The long-term success of any organization depends upon management's successful use of analytical and conceptual skills to plan and guide the organization's growth and future direction.

EXERCISE 1.2
In the situation described earlier, Liz must undertake a number of tasks to reorganize the circulation desk schedule. Divide these tasks into the broad general skills groups discussed above.

Human skills

Technical skills

Conceptual skills

Management Levels

Of course, not all managers spend the same amount of time on the four functions or use the needed skills in the same proportions. Generally, the functions and skills required depend upon the managers' levels and the kinds of work they do. Broadly, these levels are as follows.

Front-Line Managers

Front-line managers or supervisors oversee the work of a small number of staff, not other managers, and have limited authority.

These managers are concerned with:
- *leading* to build team spirit and motivation
- *controlling* to ensure that deadlines are met and clients given satisfactory service
- *organizing* to ensure smooth flowing processes
- *planning* of day-to-day activities.

They need a high level of technical expertise or competence in the work of the team, since they may have to provide technical solutions and make decisions concerning the nature of that work.

Human skills are also important in maintaining team motivation and making staff feel supported and nurtured. Conceptual skills are less important at this level, given the limited involvement of the front-line manager in long-term planning and decision-making.

These are examples of front-line managers:
head of circulation, stack supervisor, manager of a digitization team.

Middle Managers

Middle managers direct the activities of other managers as well as staff. They are often responsible for planning policy and procedures and may have budgetary and staffing responsibilities.

These managers:

- *plan* improvements to practices and procedures
- *organize* in the longer term to ensure that sufficient resources are available, e.g., staffing
- *control* to ensure that plans and procedures are working as anticipated
- *motivate* to set the climate in which effective teams can grow.

They need a lower level of technical expertise or competence in the work of the team, as they may often rely on advice from front-line managers in order to make decisions. However, they must be capable of properly interpreting that advice. Human skills are important to ensure that individuals and teams understand the reasons for decisions and actions and are motivated to achieve departmental or organization goals. Conceptual skills become more important at this level as the involvement in longer-term, more complex planning increases.

 These are examples of middle managers:
manager of a special library, section head in a larger information center.

Senior Managers

Senior or top managers direct the activities of the organization as a whole. They are responsible for the long-term direction and corporate morale of an institution.

Top-level managers look at long-term threats and opportunities for the organization and are concerned with future directions, rather than day-to-day planning. They are involved in initiating or approving changes to practices and procedures; delegating authority to organize resources; and ensuring that appropriate control measures are built into all long-term plans. Finally, senior managers set the 'atmosphere' for an organization that encourages staff to develop their full potential.

At this level, managers are unlikely to have a high level of technical expertise in the work of the organization but rely upon advice from lower-level staff. Human skills are very important to ensure that lower-level management and staff are 'brought along' with the aims of the organization. Conceptual skills are the most important attribute at this level, with managers doing long-term planning and having to make assumptions regarding complex future events. A clear vision for any organization is essential for its long-term success.

 These are examples of senior managers:
head of a public library system, university librarian.

EXERCISE 1.3

In a large university library, consider each level of management and the responsibilities of each. List some of the areas you feel may be of concern at each level. For example:

The university librarian will need to plan for

Middle management may need to cope with staffing issues in relation to

Front-line supervisors will have to deal with

SCENARIO

In a small group, consider the following case study as if you were the manager or supervisor. Use the discussion in this chapter as a guide and brainstorm other ideas and options. You are expected to deliver a practical and workable solution that is in the best interests of the staff and the organization.

Sandy is employed by a contract cataloging service, the Cataloging Company, to undertake cataloging work in a government department library. Her work requires her to undertake original cataloging of some in-house published material not held elsewhere. This is part of a retrospective cataloging project aimed at putting some very old material into the database.

Sandy is paid on a piecework basis, $10 for every item she fully catalogs, regardless of whether it is easy or complex. Sandy is not happy with this arrangement since this cataloging is very complex and time-consuming, resulting in much lower wages for Sandy than for members of the permanent library staff, who are often engaged in less demanding work.

Sandy has discussed this situation with her employer, who claims to be unable to change the arrangement at the moment due to the nature of the contract with the department. The flexibility of the arrangement—she can work any 30 hours per week she chooses—suits her very well, and she is reluctant to leave, despite the low pay. She does, however, feel frustrated and irritated with the work and her employer.

Consider how well the management of the Cataloging Company has exercised its conceptual, human, and technical skills in managing this contract. As Sandy, how would you ensure that your concerns are taken into account, if another contract comes up for negotiation?

📖 References and Further Reading

Arns, J.W. & C. Price, *To market, to market: the supervisory skills and managerial competencies most valued by new library supervisors*. Chicago, American Library Association, 2007.

Chang, Amy & Kawanna Bright, 'Changing roles of middle managers in academic libraries', *Library Management* 33:4/5, 2012, pages 213 – 220.

DiMattia, Ernie, 'Leadership vs management', *Library Journal* 14 January 2013. http://lj.libraryjournal.com/2013/01/opinion/focus-on-leadership-and-management/leadership-vs-management-focus-on-leadership-and-management/

Fedeczko, Joyce L., 'Managing in the middle: the librarian's handbook', *Library Management* 36:4/5, 2015, pages 381 – 382.

Fitsimmons, Gary. 2014. 'On being a good library supervisor', *The Bottom Line: Managing Library Finances* 27:1, 2014, pages 14 – 16.

Pymm, Bob & Damian Lodge, *Can evidence based research methods assist library managers in becoming better managers?* [online], 2005. http://conferences.alia.org.au/ebl2005/Pymm.pdf

School Library Monthly, *Library management blog*, [online]. http://blog.schoollibrarymedia.com/index.php/category/library-management/

Sunrise, *What skills does a manager need?* [online]. http://sunrisepage.com/manage/skilmana.htm

Thrasher, Harwell. 2009. *How to become a manager: 13 skills you'll need*, [online]. http://blog.makingitclear.com/2009/06/24/managerskills/

Topper, Elisa F. 2007. 'Supervisor's attitude and employee's performance', *New Library World*, 108:9/10, 2007, pages 460 – 462.

VEA Australia, *Management roles: planning, organizing, leading, controlling*. Youtube (2m31sec), 2012. https://www.youtube.com/watch?v=WhCPqk9bAtg

CHAPTER TWO
The External Environment

Introduction

All organizations exist within an environment that affects the work they do and how they do it. They also generate their own internal environment, which affects the 'feel' of the place and influences how the organization runs. Understanding these environments and their impact is vital to ensure that planning, particularly for the long term, takes into account as many of the variables as possible. It is therefore important that a manager gather information from as wide a range of sources as possible in order to make reasoned decisions.

External Environment

The external environment comprises everything over which the organization has little or no control, but which may affect the way it does its business. Listed below are just some of these factors:

- government policies
- social values
- demographics and geography
- tradition
- the market
- changes in technology
- competitors
- suppliers.

Government Policies

Federal, state, or local government policies can all have a very direct impact upon the way an organization operates. These may include:

- budgetary measures such as reduced funding or increased taxes and charges for services—e.g. increased state or federal tax; increased salary scales for employees
- changes in philosophy such as the introduction and promotion of user fees—e.g., if museums and galleries were instructed to charge entrance fees
- support or the withdrawal of support for particular industries—e.g. the national or state library increases fees for inter library loans
- staff ceilings or hiring freezes in government departments—e.g., closures of public schools result in fewer school libraries
- social legislation and policy that may impact upon an organization—e.g., if federal agencies were no longer required to follow a centralized salary scale but could set their own pay rates.

Many libraries and information centers are supported by government funding either directly or indirectly. Examples of directly funded services are government departmental libraries and information services; indirectly funded libraries include university or college libraries that may be affected if funding to the parent organization is reduced. Changes to policies and practices can therefore have a big impact on their nature and their ability to deliver services.

Social Values

The values and interests of any society are constantly evolving as tastes and fashions change. These are difficult to predict and monitor, often because they are seen very much through the eyes of individuals, who are affected by their upbringing and view of the world. However, objective consideration of issues is necessary if their impact is to be assessed and if the organization is to cope with the change. The sorts of issues may include:

- changing tastes, so that demand for certain goods or services may be affected—e.g., in public libraries, patrons may no longer borrow many westerns, but crime fiction may increase in popularity
- growing sophistication of audiences due to exposure to high-quality, high-cost products—e.g., blockbuster art or museum exhibitions may make a local history museum relatively unattractive to visitors
- changing habits and lifestyles, which make traditional opening hours less useful to patrons than they once were—e.g., a storefront library in a shopping mall may need to open longer hours and at weekends to meet increasing demand for its services; a university library may need to provide 24/7 availability to meet student demand for out of hours access
- growth in vocal pressure groups with specific demands—e.g., an environmental group may open an information center to generate support for a particular issue.

Demographics and Geography

Population changes and physical location can also have a big impact on the operations of an organization. Changes that may occur include:

- changes to traffic patterns, resulting in a reduction in passing traffic—e.g., a tourist information center that is no longer on a main road after a bypass opens
- the opening of new facilities, shifting the center of activity—e.g., a new shopping mall may take customers away from the traditional center of town where the public library is located
- the redevelopment of an inner city area, changing its population—e.g., the local public library may find it no longer has an active seniors group
- changes in the ethnic makeup of an area—e.g., a public branch library in what was a predominantly Greek neighborhood now needs staff with Asian languages
- aging populations in some suburbs—e.g., an older suburb with a shrinking population may find its public library branch replaced by a bookmobile service.

Tradition

The history of an institution and its traditions shape the way it is today and will continue to influence its development. For example:

- a university library that has always given academic staff a six-month borrowing period may find this difficult to reduce without opposition
- the practice of traditionally performing all cataloging in-house may mean that consideration of a cost-effective option to outsource some or all of the cataloging load will meet with resistance

- the replacement of a traditional reference desk with a 'meet and greet' service approach supported by roaming help staff may require a substantial level of difficult readjustment for those involved.

Thus, custom and tradition can be powerful forces that resist change. Managers need to be aware of this fact, and take it into account in planning.

The Market

The market for the service being offered can change without warning. These things may be very difficult to predict but must be considered regularly, as they can have a major impact on the organization. Situations that can occur include:

- a special library serving a government department may find after a reshuffle of government responsibilities that the department has been abolished or combined with another. To survive, the library will have to respond to a different set of users with different demands
- with the closure of a local welfare office, the local public library may be expected to deal with an increase in those seeking information on their rights and benefits
- with increasing availability of library resources online, a university library may find a decrease in the number of face-to-face reference questions, along with a demand for more complex online reference assistance
- the growth in a 24/7 service ethic within the academic library world may result in student expectations at a small college of their library staying open all night too.

With the advances being brought about by technology, and rapidly increasing client expectations, changes in demand occur more quickly than in the past. Monitoring and anticipating these changes is an important part of the manager's role.

Changes in Technology

Rapid technological change has had a major impact on how libraries and information services deliver their products and services. The Internet has opened up access to vast amounts of previously unobtainable data and has greatly improved the manner in which information can be delivered and the ease with which traditional library users can now undertake their own searching. Examples include:

- remote access to catalogs and content from outside the organization via local and international networks, which may lead to increased demand on the collection (e.g., via interlibrary loan) and thus on staff and other resources
- an increasingly varied and complex array of resources, acquired through complicated licensing agreements and accessed via a range of different computer interfaces, which staff have to become proficient in using
- gradual replacement of physical collections by online materials, which may cause difficulties for some users and will also increase the need for larger, more sophisticated computer networks and Wi-Fi availability within the library
- demanding clients who are familiar with the resources of the Web and expect a far higher level of service than before
- the impact on staff having to adapt to changing software and delivery platforms that call for continual training and updating of their skills.

These changes bring opportunities for providing better service, but also raise issues for an organization regarding the need for capital expenditure on equipment, training, etc. that must be allocated, possibly at the expense of other activities.

Competitors

Competitors may emerge that do some or all of the organization's traditional tasks. While competition can have beneficial effects in encouraging an organization to define more clearly its role, customers, markets, products and services, it can also have serious effects on its long-term viability in a small or fixed market that cannot expand to cope with the newcomer. Thus:

- Internet access and other end-user searching may reduce demand for access to traditional materials and possibly reduce reference inquiries and physical access to the library or information center building
- independent information specialists may undertake research or processing tasks, such as cataloging, at a rate that is perceived to be cheaper than that of the library with all its attendant overheads
- with the growth in outsourcing as a principle for dealing with specialized activities, some in-house expertise may no longer be maintained—e.g., a German-language cataloger may no longer be permanently employed, with all such cataloging outsourced and paid for at a piecework rate
- the use of 'the crowd' to assist on tasks usually undertaken by paid staff—e.g., the enhancement of cataloging records, particularly for newly digitized material, may lead to a loss of paid staff positions.

Increasingly, governments are encouraging competition in order to increase efficiency and reduce costs. For management this trend represents a challenge to the traditional approach which, if not handled correctly, can be disastrous.

Suppliers

An organization's suppliers may go out of business, change ownership and attitudes, or simply move into other fields and no longer provide an effective service. If this is done without sufficient notice it can create serious problems. For example:

- a serial supplier or database aggregator may add or drop titles from its bundled subscription packages, which means the library is paying for titles it does not want or is missing out on titles it needs
- a specialist supplier of packing material used by a major archive may suddenly raise prices or otherwise change the conditions by which it supplies materials (e.g., payment in advance) that force the organization to cope with unplanned budget changes, or to look for other suppliers in a limited market
- suppliers can change invoicing practices, give or refuse credit, set minimum orders, charge high shipping and handling costs for small deliveries, etc.

Despite an increasingly competitive market, there may still be many difficulties for managers in quickly changing suppliers due to the nature of the materials involved. They must take care when entering into contracts with suppliers, taking into account the difficulty of moving to another source if problems should arise.

Managers may feel frustrated over their inability to change or even to influence many of the situations described above. However, it is their responsibility to consider these and related issues in their longer-term planning and to put in place strategies and practices that will assist in coping with them if they come to pass.

EXERCISE 2.1
For a library with which you are familiar (e.g., your workplace, university, college, public, or school library), consider each of the factors in its external environment listed below. Note under each heading the factors you expect may have to be considered and how they may affect the way the library provides its service.
Can you think of any other important factors?

Government policies

Social values

Demographics and geography

Tradition

The market

Changes in technology

Competition

Suppliers

Assessing the Environment

As a way of evaluating the environment within which an organization operates, managers have developed a process known as SWOT analysis. SWOT stands for:

- **S**trengths
- **W**eaknesses
- **O**pportunities
- **T**hreats.

Strengths and weaknesses refer to the internal environment of an organization (and are discussed in the following chapter); opportunities and threats refer to the external environment.

Opportunities

'Opportunities' denotes those events or factors in the external environment that may offer real potential for the organization. For libraries and related institutions, examples include the following:

- with the growth of interest by the over-60s in understanding social networking applications or simpler Internet applications, public libraries in particular have the opportunity to develop this market segment by providing training and advice to this particular demographic
- major events can provide opportunities that may benefit information providers. For instance, the centenary of the outbreak of World War I has seen a massive effort to digitize relevant service records, photographs, films and other material related to the conflict in order to provide an interested public easy access to these collections
- the ease with which images and text can be captured and digitized makes the exploitation of pictorial and other materials a simple matter. Photograph collections, diaries, oral histories, newspapers etc. are being digitized at a great rate around the world. Exploiting these previously difficult to access collections is now a major role for virtually all information organizations—from the tiniest local history collection to the biggest national archive
- with the growing acceptance of commercialization, sponsorship and user-fee services within the information professions, opportunities arise to establish self-funding enterprises attached to existing organizations to exploit resources and expertise.

Threats

'Threats' refers to events or factors in the external environment that may prove detrimental to the growth and effectiveness of the organization. For libraries and related institutions, threats include:

- the growth of the Internet and its use as a primary resource for information (and recreation) by a large number of people. The perception that physical libraries are no longer required is growing, and could impact negatively when governments of all type are looking to reduce budgets
- increased demand for non-book materials by library patrons. These include electronic books in a range of formats, DVDs, audio books (again in a range of formats), computer software, and even the hardware related to some of these materials. Especially in public libraries, this demand increases the strain on limited budgets. How many of these should the library carry, how many publicly accessible computer

terminals should be made available, and how much do these facilities and services cross over with commercial providers?

- falling exchange rates and escalating journal prices, which make it difficult for academic libraries to maintain subscription levels
- demands for reduced government spending and altered priorities that adversely affect funding
- burgeoning output, both print and electronic, making selection increasingly difficult and time consuming with many organizations now looking at 'patron driven' approaches to selection. Otherwise known as 'just in time', this refers to the approach, which works well with e-publications, whereby materials are not acquired until actually asked for. This is both an opportunity—money is not spent on material for which there is no demand—but is also a threat as the library is very much dependent upon the supplier and its pricing and speed of response.

Opportunities and threats have always existed and all organizations have to cope with them through effective management. In the current climate of ever faster change, foreseeing and correctly evaluating the impact of changes is no easy task.

Identifying change factors and developing strategies to take advantage of the possibilities, or minimize the threat they pose, is a crucial part of any manager's long-term planning.

EXERCISE 2.2

The Digital Library Federation is a consortium of libraries and related agencies that research learning in areas of digital delivery and the public good. Through its members, the DLF provides leadership for libraries broadly by

- *identifying standards and 'best practices' for digital collections and network access*
- *coordinating leading-edge research and development in libraries' use and preservation of digital data and*
- *providing support and education in the field.*

Consider the coming five years. What do you see as:

The opportunities it may have?

The threats it will have to face?

The strategies it might employ to take advantage of opportunities and minimize threats?

SCENARIO

In a small group, consider the following case study as if you were the manager or supervisor. Use the discussion in this chapter as a guide and brainstorm other ideas and options. You are expected to deliver a practical and workable solution that is in the best interests of the staff and the organization.

As an elderly volunteer in an inner-city public library, Roland is happy with his two mornings a week shelving and generally tidying around the reading and reference area, sorting out the newspapers and magazines that readers generally leave in a mess. He has been doing this for many years now and has noticed that some books and authors that used to be popular no longer seem to be taken off the shelves. Certain magazines, once the mainstay of the reading area, are rarely read.

Roland noted some of his observations and presented them to Deb, the public services librarian and his nominal boss. In a quiet moment Deb considered Roland's comments and began thinking over the changes in this inner-city library since it was established in 1947. She had been asked to do a presentation to a local seniors' group in a month's time and decided to cover the changes in the area since 1947 and how they have, directly or indirectly, affected the library and its collection.

As Deb, where would you start in your research for this presentation and what sort of information do you think you would need?

📖 References and Further Reading

Canuel, Robin & Chad Crichton, 'Canadian academic libraries and the mobile web'. *New Library World* 112:3/4, 2011, pages 107 – 120.

Castiglione, James, 'Environmental scanning: an essential tool for twenty-first century librarianship', *Library Review* 57:7, 2008, pages 528 – 536.

JISC, *Managing strategic activity: Prioritisation: PESTLE and SWOT analysis*, [online], 2014. https://www.jisc.ac.uk/guides/managing-strategic-activity/prioritisation

LeoIsaac.com, *Environmental factors in strategic planning*, [online]. http://www.leoisaac.com/planning/strat016.htm

Queensland Government. Business and Industry Portal, *Example SWOT analysis*, [online], 2013. https://www.business.qld.gov.au/business/starting/market-customer-research/swot-analysis/example-swot-analysis

CHAPTER THREE
The Internal Environment

Introduction

Like the external environment, the internal environment that develops formally and informally in any organization has an impact on how it operates. Unlike the external environment, where the organization has very little control, the internal environment is shaped and influenced by the organization itself.

However, not everything in the organization is directly controllable. Even in the smallest workplaces, there can arise both a formal environment (that evolves in the direction the organization would wish) and an informal environment over which it has little control, that grows out of staff interests, values, and concerns.

 *The product of all these forces is commonly known as the **culture** of an organization.*

The Formal Environment

The formal internal environment comprises the systems developed and implemented by the organization to meet its long-term goals. These systems evolve, and in any dynamic organization they are regularly reviewed, updated, and evaluated in an effort to manage the effects of changes caused by the external environment.

For example, if governments change the rules regarding the employment of ongoing, full time staff, making it more difficult to recruit permanent people, there is little the organization can do to affect this legislation. However, it may be able to change its internal rules and procedures to take account of the government's intentions, while at the same time allowing the organization to still achieve its own goals.

Some of the systems and processes that help create the organization's formal internal environment are:

- management planning systems
- policies and practices
- organizational structure
- union presence
- service or product
- management style
- recruitment and personnel policies
- staff skills
- technology
- budgets.

Management Planning Systems

Management planning systems should involve staff in developing strategic and operational plans. By involving all the staff in developing these plans, a greater understanding of the plans is fostered—and possibly a greater commitment to their achievement. In addition, staff will be encouraged to put forward their own ideas and vision that may contribute to the long-term success of the organization.

Policies and Practices

Policies, practices, and procedures are created in all organizations to ensure that work is completed according to certain guidelines and standards. Such policies and practices may include practical issues such as opening and closing times, whether interlibrary loans are charged or not, and whether an item is acquired in more than one format (e.g., print and electronic). Broader issues may cover staff recruitment practices, collection development policies, and collection security measures.

Organizational Structure

Organizational structure and shape influence the flow of information throughout the institution. Whether departments are based on geography (e.g., state offices), or function (e.g., reference, technical services) may affect the way they work. Managers closely involved in the day-to-day work are more likely to influence that area than a manager remote from the workplace.

Union Presence

Whether a workplace is unionized or not will help shape the internal environment. If the unions are seen as powerful in a particular industry or organization, they can have a very strong influence on its formal environment.

Service or Product

The nature of the product or service delivered by an organization has a direct impact on its structure and work environment. Thus a simple product being mass-produced (e.g., a McDonalds' hamburger) calls for staff to follow a clearly defined set of rules—there is no room for individual creativity or initiative. This is quite different from, for example, the reference desk in an academic library, where staff will have procedural guidelines to help them in their day-to-day work but the nature of their job means they need to show judgment, exercise initiative, make decisions and prioritize tasks using their individual experience and knowledge of the field.

Management Style

The style adopted by senior management influences the internal environment of the organization. A formal, traditional, and hierarchical style of management will tend to limit initiative and spontaneity and will discourage contributions from others in meetings where the manager is putting forward his or her ideas. In contrast, a more informal, decentralized management approach passes responsibility further down the line, encouraging initiative, action, ideas, and suggestions. However, this can increase risks to the organization, since some of these initiatives may fail and the time required to make decisions and initiate actions will inevitably be greater.

Recruitment and Personnel Policies

The method of recruiting, training, and developing employees will influence the way in which staff members are assimilated into the culture of an organization. These policies can have a major impact on how staff adapt to their new environment and build loyalty to their employer.

Positive policies that try to match people to jobs, listen to their concerns and interests, and take a real interest in their career development will help build commitment and support for the organization, as well as provide a skilled workforce as a basis for improving productivity and quality. The nature of the employment relationship—from a short term contract to a permanent ongoing position—will also influence an individual's commitment and view of their employer and the workplace.

Staff Skills

Skills possessed by staff affect the nature and quality of work performed. Thus experience and training are important to ensure that the organization gains the most benefit from its staff resources. Keeping experienced staff, with their skills and corporate knowledge, influences a culture but at the same time, bringing in new staff, with new ideas and viewpoints, can also have a positive effect.

Technology

Technological development in the organization can impact on its environment. At its simplest, it may affect only the manner in which work is done and the practices and procedures required to perform the task. At a more complex level, new technology may transform organizational dynamics by altering the way work is done, creating more isolated tasks, requiring some workers to develop different skills, changing the staff mix to emphasize new skills at the expense of traditional knowledge, and so on.

Budgets

The manner in which budget dollars are allocated toward particular tasks will direct most of the organization's activities and thus affect its culture. For example, it may be decided to reduce monograph acquisitions to cover the increasing cost of serial subscriptions, or to replace physical items with electronic versions which will impact upon the physical space as well as the tasks involved with acquisition and lending.

EXERCISE 3.1

Stephanie is the manager of a large community information center with a permanent staff of 5 and over 30 volunteers. As well as helping visitors who drop in, they provide an active online advice and assistance service. Consider the points below and note how they might impact on the 'shape' of the internal environment of the center.

Can you think of any other factors over which Stephanie has control that would influence staff harmony and morale at the center?

Policies, practices, and procedures

Organizational structure

Nature of the service

Management style

Technology

Budget

Other

The Informal Environment

This environment grows in organizations without any direct attempt by managers to encourage it—and often despite their attempts to control it. It is rarely clearly defined but changes according to a large number of factors, including the makeup of individual work groups. Changing a negative informal environment into a positive one is one of management's harder tasks.

Factors contributing to the informal environment include:

- tradition
- personal needs and interests
- bureaucracy
- charismatic leaders.

Tradition

Tradition is a powerful force which, by its nature, takes much time and energy to change. Work groups used to functioning in a particular manner may find it difficult to accept new approaches, or even new members into the team. The strength of tradition should not be underestimated—which often makes introducing change a challenging process despite the formal internal environment supporting it.

Personal Needs and Interests

Personal needs can lead individuals to have goals that differ from those of the organization, resulting in an informal environment that does not support the aims that the organization is trying to pursue. For example, a staff member dreaming of retirement may not be dedicated to providing the highest quality work but will be content with providing the bare minimum.

Bureaucracy

Bureaucratic difficulties or 'red tape' (i.e., the formal internal environment) that are perceived as slowing down or complicating various activities for no obvious benefit may be short-circuited, ignored, or belittled in an informal way. Safety standards may suffer in this way, and it is essential that management recognize this possibility and design systems based upon common sense. In addition, management needs to develop good promotion campaigns explaining why a certain practice is necessary.

Charismatic Leaders

Charismatic personalities, whatever their formal position in the organization, influence the manner and amount of work performed. Such leaders or opinion makers have to be taken into account by management seeking to implement change, and ideally should be brought 'on board' early in support of the change.

EXERCISE 3.2

In the upper-school library where Kerrie works, teachers are in the habit of taking new books as soon as they arrive in the library, often before they have been processed. Frequently, it can be a struggle to get these items returned. Often, many months pass before they come back, and occasionally the items never return. Kerrie has discussed this problem with individual teachers and the principal, but no one really takes it seriously. There seems to be an informal culture that says it's okay to take these books, and if it is a while before they come back, well, 'no big deal'. Yet students are missing out, particularly those preparing for a university education.

Using the headings below, note some of the factors influencing this informal environment and consider how easy it may be to change any of them.

Tradition

Personal needs

Bureaucracy

Charismatic leaders

Assessing the Environment

As noted in the previous chapter, it is important to assess aspects of the environment, both internal and external, in order to plan future directions properly. Those factors affecting the internal environment, both formal and informal, can be termed potential strengths and weaknesses.

Strengths

'Strengths' are those internal resources held and fostered by the organization that enable it to provide high-quality service. Collections with strong areas of specialization are among the major strengths of many libraries. Public libraries may build substantial local history collections that provide an unparalleled resource for study of a local area, and other special libraries will build collections related to their areas of interest.

Expertise and corporate knowledge among staff are usually the other major strengths of any organization that deals with information. An experienced person working in the library of a major urban newspaper with pressing deadlines each day will be a real asset in rapidly locating the appropriate reference, clipping, photograph, etc. for the next edition.

 For management, the task is first to recognize strengths in an organization. It must then ensure that any future strategies, developments, or changes take into account these strengths in order to minimize the risk that they are lost or overlooked.

Weaknesses

Weaknesses are apparent in all organizations and may be more volatile than strengths, which tend to have a measure of stability. What may be a weakness one year may be overcome quite rapidly the next. Weaknesses may cover the whole gamut of operations, including insufficiently trained staff causing dissatisfied customers, poor selection decisions leading to an unbalanced collection, inappropriate management structures, rigidity in procedures, etc.

 It can be hard for managers to recognize weaknesses in the organization, due to their closeness and commitment to its purpose. While some weaknesses may be readily overcome once recognized, identifying them and dealing with them can be difficult.

Building a Creative Environment

It should now be clear that there is no 'right' internal environment or culture. Every organization is unique and what works well in one situation may be quite inappropriate elsewhere or at another time. However, one aspect of the internal environment should be encouraged in virtually any type of organization—creativity.

For managers, building an environment where creativity is encouraged and rewarded can be challenging and threatening. Yet there can be major benefits for the organization if it is pursued.

Paust (2005) outlines a number of approaches managers should adopt in encouraging this type of organizational culture:

- Invest in employee development and growth by providing training and related opportunities as an integral part of staff development and support. Identify and build on individual strengths.
- Acknowledge staff concerned in the development and implementation of new ideas and ensure they are properly recognized and rewarded for their efforts.
- Create a sense of ownership and accountability in employees while at the same time encouraging the sharing of ideas and team brainstorming.
- Promote a culture that acknowledges the need for continuous improvement while at the same time developing an acceptance of change in staff.
- Build confidence in staff and accept that not all ideas will work out in practice. Managers need to plan and be prepared for innovations that do not live up to expectations.
- Explain objectives clearly to staff and give them the freedom and responsibility to achieve them within the constraints and philosophy of the organization.

SCENARIO

In a small group, consider the following case study as if you were the manager or supervisor. Use the discussion in this chapter as a guide and brainstorm other ideas and options. You are expected to deliver a practical and workable solution that is in the best interests of the staff and the organization.

Andrew works as the librarian in a medium-sized legal practice. In this role he supports the legal staff in tracking down a wide range of (usually) nonlegal information to assist in their case preparation.

Andrew has found it a busy job serving five attorneys, with some of the work stimulating and interesting, while with other parts he sometimes wonders how useful the information for which he is searching could be.

The managing partners are looking at cutting costs and have asked Andrew to justify the continuation of his position. They candidly tell him they are thinking of abolishing it as 'the lawyers can do their own hack work'.

Consider the strengths and weaknesses of the information service Andrew provides. Prepare a report outlining them with the conclusion that the strengths very much outweigh the weaknesses. Make any assumptions you need to, but explain when you have done so.

References and Further Reading

Castiglione, James, 'Facilitating employee creativity in the library environment: an important managerial concern for library administrators', *Library Management* 29:3, 2008, pages 159 – 172.

Curzon, Susan Carol, *Managing change: a how-to-do-it manual for librarians.* Rev. ed., New York, Neal-Schuman, 2006

Gutsche, Betha. Coping with continual motion. *Library Journal* March 1st, 2010. http://lj.libraryjournal.com/2010/03/professional-reading/coping-with-continual-motion/

Paust, Michael, *Best practices for building an innovative work culture,* [online]. http://www.ebizq.net/topics/web_content_management/features/5558.html

Queensland government. Business and Industry Portal, *Management styles*, [online], 2013. https://www.business.qld.gov.au/business/employing/managing-staff/management-styles

CHAPTER FOUR
Organizational Structure and Design

Introduction
Any organization that grows beyond a small family business must have a formal structure indicating lines of authority, specialist activities, and relationships within the organization.

As organizations grow, so does the complexity of their structure. This structure should be able to illustrate to those outside the institution the way in which different work activities relate to each other, where responsibilities lie, and how communication flows in the organization. An organization's structure is often shown as a diagram or chart.

Structure is affected by a number of variables including:
- long-term strategy
- the size and age of an organization
- technology
- the product or service delivered
- the external environment.

eg An example of how structure is affected by technology is the change in responsibilities that has been driven by the online sharing of cataloging information and subsequent decline in original cataloging in most organizations. This has had a significant impact on workplace hierarchies and relationships and the way in which staffing resources are allocated. Structures within organizations have had to change to take full advantage of these advances driven by technology.

As organizations and their goals evolve, so does the structure best suited to achieving these goals. What worked well ten years ago may no longer be useful and may even hinder the institution in fulfilling its mission today.

Organizational Designs
There is no single best structure appropriate to all organizations. As noted above, a number of factors influence what, at any time, is the most effective structure. However, at their basis, all structures must provide a guide as to how work is distributed. Once the organization has moved from being simply an owner with a handful of employees at the same level to one where there are supervisors or intermediate managers, the need for a more formal structure becomes apparent.

Traditional organizational structures are often referred to as **mechanistic designs**. These are the simplest to implement and, depending upon the nature of the work and the organization's needs, may be the most appropriate.

Two types of mechanistic design structures are:
- functional design
- product design.

Functional Design

This design uses a structure that reflects the nature of the work. For example, a traditional library environment may have a structure as shown in the diagram below.

The advantage of this structure is its concentration of specialist expertise in a particular area, leading to well-trained staff, potential career paths, and possible economies of scale by concentrating each task in one area. It is also easier to manage than more complex structures by providing clear, discrete functions for each area.

The structure's main drawback lies with the difficulty of ensuring that each section pursues overall library and organizational goals, rather than those of its own section. Thus the Cataloging Department may pursue policies that maximize its effectiveness but do not help Public Services do its work, or vice versa.

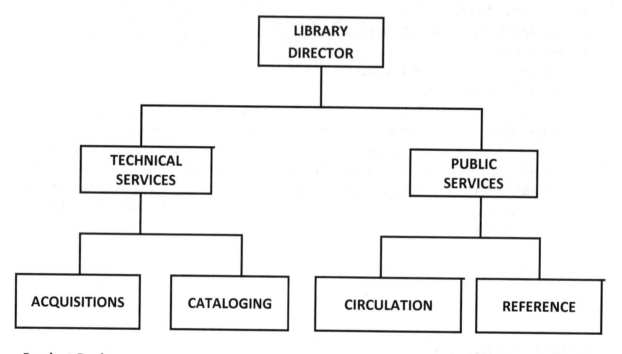

Product Design

Product design uses a structure that reflects the different types of materials handled. This structure is illustrated in the chart below.

Complex organizations such as a large academic library, museum, or archives may use this structure to encourage specialist expertise in an area. Again, the nature of this division of responsibilities may lead to a concern with the specific, rather than the 'big picture', but does encourage completeness in dealing with a particular product or service.

For instance, in the example shown, all work concerning audiovisual records—such as acquisition, cataloging, and reference work—would be done in the same section. Such an arrangement will encourage a high level of coordination among staff handling these records, lead to a depth of expertise among the staff, and allow a high standard of service to users. It also provides staff members with opportunities to move within their areas of specialization, say from cataloging to reference work, with relative ease.

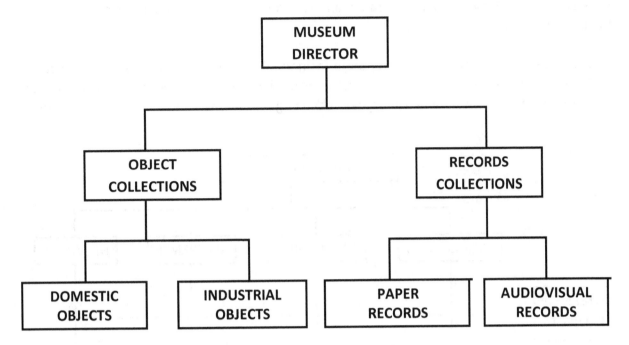

The major disadvantage relates to a possible duplication of resources and difficulties in coordinating and applying organization-wide standards, as each section oversees the work of its own catalogers, collection development officers, reference staff, etc.

Organic Design
These traditional mechanistic organization types have been criticized for their rigidity and tendency to promote local cultures rather than a broader, organizational culture. In order to overcome some of these perceived problems, more flexible groupings have been tried in recent years. They have been termed **organic designs** or structures and attempt to combine the strengths of the mechanistic structures while overcoming some of their drawbacks. Examples are:
- matrix structures
- network structures
- project group or task force structures.

Matrix Structures
Matrix structures aim to combine the advantages of the functional and product structures described above and to overcome their disadvantages by establishing an organization where functional specialists become involved in specific projects or programs related to the organization's overall goals. In this model, staff answer to two managers, one concerned with the functional area and one managing the project. It requires a different management approach that emphasizes flexibility, open communication, and cooperation between managers as well as staff.

An example of how this model works is shown below. Two projects are shown, one on maximizing effective use of social media and one on developing a temporary exhibition space in the library. The project teams draw on staff from the functional areas of Acquisitions, Cataloging, Public Programs, and Network/IT Services, which form the basis of the library's structure.

The nature of the matrix should be apparent from the illustration. As projects are completed, staff move on to new activities, and the matrix changes its components. This style of structure is particularly suitable to the ever-changing environments that many organizations face today.

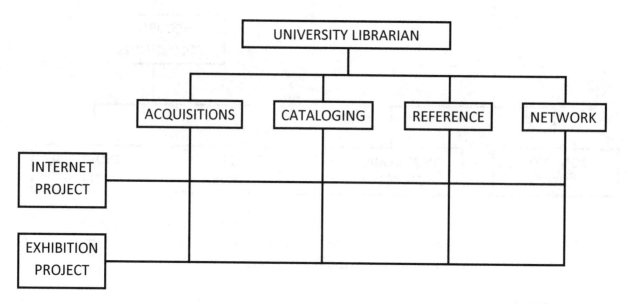

The advantages of this approach are the flexibility it offers to meet unforeseen demands and the cross-training (i.e., multi-skilling) and development possibilities it offers staff by providing opportunities in activities outside their normal work. Involving staff in tasks that are not related to their usual focus gives them a wider understanding of organizational needs, and by broadening their 'parochial' view of the work environment provides a significant opportunity for personal development.

The disadvantage is the demand it places on management to cope with increased complexity and the need for greater cooperation and coordination. It also places pressures on staff, some of whom may be uncomfortable with the challenge it offers.

Other Organic Structures

There are other organic structures, but their applicability to the library and information environment is probably limited. Examples include:

- a *network structure* based upon the premise that virtually all functions are outsourced to other organizations, with a small management core coordinating and directing activities
- a *project group or task force structure*, suitable for dealing with a particular situation (e.g., the introduction of a new library management system), but still requiring an underlying permanent structure within which to operate.

Note that this discussion has concentrated on the formal organizational structure as devised by management. However, in all organizations there exists an informal structure where the actual information and work flows may well depart from the formal hierarchy, due to the social nature of work and the relationships among staff. These informal structures will always exist and it is important to take them into account if the formal structure is to be revised or a new structure implemented.

EXERCISE 4.1

For any library or information center with which you are familiar, draw up its organizational structure and, using the headings below, discuss how this structure helps the organization perform its role. Decide which of the above structures it most closely resembles and consider whether an alternative would be possible.

Organization structure chart

Performing the work effectively and efficiently

Meeting staff needs

Meeting user needs

Alternative structures

Organizational Structure, Work Design, and Job Satisfaction

The choice of structure has an impact on the nature of work in the organization, as well as having a major impact on the levels of job satisfaction felt by managers and employees. The following three key factors, emerging from the structure adopted by an organization, impact upon the way in which the work is performed and the level of satisfaction felt by all staff:

- nature of the work
- teams and project groups
- span of control.

Nature of the Work

Under traditional, mechanistic structures, work has generally been of a routine, predictable nature. For example, working in an acquisitions section or copy cataloging unit entails performing a well-defined set of tasks which, once mastered, become routine. Opportunities for creativity are limited in these structures. Some staff appreciate the routine of the work but others become bored. Promotional opportunities outside the area become restricted due to the level of specialization.

Use of a matrix or similar structure offers opportunities to develop options for job enrichment and skills enhancement that provide more challenge for staff. It also encourages lateral thinking about how tasks are done, and fosters creativity and innovation in work practices that may benefit staff members and the organization. This wider range of opportunities builds staff confidence, skills, and knowledge—resulting in increased promotional opportunities and broader career paths.

Teams and Project Groups

The use of teams and project groups allows a high degree of task identity and commitment, while offering variety in the work performed. For staff in large departments such as an Information Services area in a major academic library, the work may appear to be never-ending. Providing the opportunity to work on discrete tasks, where the results are clearly evident, can be a powerful motivational experience. The result will be greater staff satisfaction and, again, increased skills and knowledge and improved future prospects.

Span of Control

The span of control associated with any management structure relates to the number of staff supervised by a manager. If the work is of a structured, routine nature, or if staff have been given significant levels of responsibility, the span of control exercised by a manager may be quite large and still work successfully. However, staff access to management will be limited and the impact on morale has to be considered when broadening the span of control.

 Smaller spans of control result in greater staff/management interaction but impose a cost on the organization.

The Learning Organization

Handy (1998) and others suggest that the typical 21st century organization may have a small core of staff who oversee the work of sub-contractors, temporary employees part-time workers, agency temps and outsourced activities. This allows the organization to adapt rapidly to new circumstances.

The concept of a 'learning organization' has also been proposed. This means that the organization creates systems to encourage all employees to develop their knowledge and skills and improve efficiency and effectiveness in all respects. With this approach, flexibility and adaptability are 'built in' to the core of the organization, and staff can cope with change. Team learning and a shared vision become building blocks for such an organization.

Since change (evolutionary and revolutionary) is now endemic to the library and information industries, some or all of the strategies proposed in the learning organization philosophy can be (and are being) usefully adopted by managers of library and information agencies.

 EXERCISE 4.2

In order to emphasize the differences that the formal structure can make in completing a task, undertake the following activity in a group.

Select one person to act as the manager, who has the task of communicating to the staff (the rest of the group) how to draw the following diagram (from Kolb, Rubin, and McIntyre, p. 433):

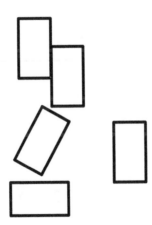

This exercise has to be done twice. In the first situation the manager stands with his/her back to the group and tries to describe what the group must do. The manager is not allowed to use pictures (only verbal communication) and the staff (group) can ask no questions.

The second approach has the manager face the group and verbally explain the diagram again. However, this time the group can ask questions of the manager and of each other.

The first approach approximates a formal structure where instructions are given by managers with little staff participation and where there is no communication between sections.

The second approach approximates a less formal structure, with an open network where managers discuss tasks with staff, and staff communicate with each other across sections.

Experiments using this exercise have found that approach 1 is considerably faster. The manager sends the message and completes the instructions quite quickly, whereas approach 2 takes much longer. However, approach 2 provides a far higher accuracy level. In addition, in approach 1 no one except the manager feels very satisfied with the process; in approach 2 staff morale and enthusiasm are generally high.

While this exercise is simplistic, it does indicate the importance of cross-communication in organizations, both upward and sideways. While there is a cost (increased time), the end result will usually be a better job. It is therefore a manager's responsibility to assess the nature of the task and adopt an approach appropriate to its needs.

SCENARIO

In a small group, consider the following case study as if you were the manager or supervisor. Use the discussion in this chapter as a guide and brainstorm other ideas and options. You are expected to deliver a practical and workable solution that is in the best interests of the staff and the organization.

Jessica has worked as the head of the Cataloging Section in the State/Provincial Library for nearly five years, supervising about ten staff. For most of that time she has enjoyed the work and found it challenging and fulfilling. Lately though, she has been concerned that productivity is falling and morale and enthusiasm are low. The two other sections comprising the Technical Services Department have also reported some problems.

Jessica has discussed the situation with the other two managers, and together they feel it may be time to consider reorganization of the entire department in order to change the manner in which materials are received and processed and to change the nature of some of the jobs in order to make them less routine. This change would affect directly the work of the Cataloging Section in particular, and may mean some staff moving to other sections in the department.

How should Jessica and the other managers design and implement any changes?

References and Further Reading

Bersin, Josh, '5 keys to building a learning organization' [online], *Forbes Leadership*, January 18 2012. http://www.forbes.com/sites#/sites/joshbersin/2012/01/18/5-keys-to-building-a-learning-organization/

Bridgespan Group, 'Designing an effective organization structure', [online presentation], 2009.
http://www.bridgespan.org/getmedia/b1139597-adfe-4dd7-bbb2-ac8c67883020/Effective-Organizations_-Structural-Design.pdf.aspx

Handy, C., *The age of unreason*. New ed., Boston, Harvard Business School, 1998.

Koizumi, M., 'Transitions in public library management: from the international perspective of strategy, organizational structure, and operations', *Journal of Library Administration* 54:8, 2014.

Matthews, Joseph R., *Strategic planning and management for library managers*, Westport, Conn., Libraries Unlimited, 2005.

Nutefall, Jennifer E. & Faye A. Chadwell, 'Preparing for the 21st century: academic library realignment', *New Library World* 113:3/4, 2012.

Piper, A. & B. Doherty, 'Creating a new organizational structure for a small academic library: the merging of technical services and access services, *Technical Services Quarterly* 32:2, 2015.

CHAPTER FIVE
Planning

Introduction
One of the most important tasks undertaken by any manager is planning, whether it is for activities to be done the next day or laying out the strategic aims for the organization over the coming five years.

 A popular maxim says "most managers don't plan to fail, they fail to plan"!

For all managers, some level of formal planning, involving strategic objectives and how they are going to be achieved, is an essential part of their role. If it isn't done, the organization will drift, changes will happen haphazardly, uncertainty will be high, and staff morale will undoubtedly suffer.

All managers plan, even if only thinking at night in bed about the next day. However, it is formal planning, where objectives are thought through, discussed with others, and written down, that is considered here.

There is a hierarchy that sets the various types of organizational planning in perspective, showing how each supports and complements the other:

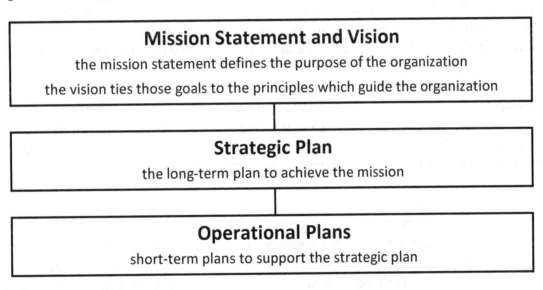

Chapters 6 and 7 of this publication discuss the components of this hierarchy in more detail.

The Planning Process
Planning is often understood as comprising two stages to support the global mission of an organization. These stages are strategic planning, dealing with long-term objectives, and operational (also called tactical) planning, dealing with day-to-day operations. Both are

inextricably linked and are discussed in the following chapters.

Generally, the following discussion applies equally to both strategic and operational planning, but with a change of emphasis depending upon which type of planning is undertaken, the nature of the plans, and the objectives being sought.

Why Plan?

Purpose and Direction

Planning is needed to give purpose and direction to an organization, to ensure that it has clear goals and objectives. Planning is particularly important as organizations increase in size and work is broken down into smaller parts. Maintaining a clear sense of purpose, common goals, and commitment across a wide range of geographically or functionally spread units will be extremely difficult unless a well-developed plan, with goals and milestones, has been developed. The plan acts as a framework within which the work of a particular section is undertaken and toward which its activities should be directed.

Conflicting Aims

Careful planning reduces the potential for overlap and conflict between sections of the organization. By defining a common purpose and targets, all areas should understand their role in helping to achieve these goals and thus limit occasions when conflict or disagreements arise.

Staff Direction

It is necessary to plan in order to ensure that staff are working toward commonly understood goals and not losing sight of the 'big picture'. It is easy for people to get caught up in the day-today aspects of a job or in the practice of professional skills, forgetting what they are ultimately trying to achieve. A clearly articulated goal and purpose that staff have helped to develop, and which is strongly promoted by senior management, will help to ensure commitment and success for the organization and to maintain focus at all levels.

Internal and External Environments

Development of a plan will encourage managers to consider external threats and opportunities and the internal strengths and weaknesses of their organization. This necessary step feeds directly into all types of planning in order to prepare realistic targets and goals that take account of the organization's environment.

Gathering and Analyzing Information

Planning provides a discipline that encourages a logical and articulated approach to decision-making. In developing any plan, management is forced to gather and analyze information, reappraise priorities, consider resource availability, and try to predict future patterns. Planning undertaken in this way will have more success than ad hoc approaches based upon the hunches or feelings of a senior manager.

Big Picture View

Planning encourages a 'big picture' view by management committed to the long-term prosperity of the organization. Medium- to long-term planning (two to five years) maps out a future for the organization and reminds management and staff that long-term health and prosperity are basic goals.

Identifying Key Areas

Planning can help to identify key areas that may help or harm the organization. These areas should become evident through the sifting of information (both internal and external to the organization) that occurs in the development of longer-term goals.

Proactive, not Reactive

Planning discourages 'fuzzy' thinking and actions by management and limits 'knee-jerk' behaviors and responses. It benefits the organization (which is not misdirected from its path by irrational responses to situations) and staff (who can have more confidence in decisions that are being made).

Control

Proper planning is essential to allow measurement and assessment of the performance of staff, management, and the organization as a whole. Without a written plan and goals, comparing actual achievements with expectations will be extremely difficult.

How to Plan Successfully

All planning has to consider the basic steps described below:

- what is to be done
- when to do it
- how to do it
- who is to do it.

What Is to Be Done

Whether long- or short-term planning is involved, it is essential that proper objectives be defined. These objectives are used as performance measures to assess whether or not, at the end of the cycle, the plan has been achieved. Thus a plan needs to consider the product or service to be delivered, together with measures to assess quantity and quality, within some sort of timeframe.

When to Do It

A time line is also essential for proper planning, and to act as a performance measure. In order to ensure the availability of the right resources at the right time, managers need to be clear about the timing of events and the order in which they will occur. One common planning procedure identifies a 'critical path' to ensure that events proceed in a logical and efficient manner in order for a complex task to be completed in the minimum time.

How to Do It

'How to do it' is part of operational planning. It is usually missing from the bigger-picture strategic planning activity, which concentrates more on outcomes than on the specifics of how to achieve them. As in the previous steps, 'how to do it' can be used as a performance measure to assess the quality of outcomes and the appropriateness of this process. It is thus useful in evaluating practices and procedures, leading to changes and improvements in systems. Depending upon the nature of the task, 'how to do it' may be quite general or very specific.

Who Is to Do It

It is essential to allocate responsibilities to oversee the implementation of long-term, strategic goals and to identify individuals to undertake specific tasks in day-to-day operational plans. Organizational structure and levels of staff abilities and training, together with an understanding of an organization's culture and ethos, will help in making the correct decisions in this area.

A Six-step Approach to Planning

Cole (2005, pp. 461-463) outlines a six-step approach to planning and makes the point that involving employees in the preparation of a plan is an important part of building their understanding and commitment to the process.

Cole's six activities are:

1. Establish goals that relate to the organization's mission, objectives, and priorities. Make sure these are specific and realistic. It must be possible to measure progress towards the goals and know when they have been achieved.

2. Note the activities that are necessary to achieve these goals and the resources required. Use meetings, brainstorming or other approaches to ensure the widest possible input into the discussion.

3. Program the activities in a logical sequence: what needs to be completed before the next step can commence? And assign responsibilities and targets as appropriate. Use planning techniques such as Gantt charts or more sophisticated software packages to assist in this process.

4. Make sure the plan is widely communicated and discussion encouraged. Be open to alterations or ready to explain why a certain approach is preferred.

5. Once the plan has been discussed and the approach confirmed, put the plan into action in a positive and enthusiastic manner.

6. Ensure progress is monitored throughout, particularly in the early days. You need to know as soon as possible if things are going wrong. At the end of the process, a formal evaluation of what worked and what didn't may be appropriate depending upon the nature and complexity of the plan.

EXERCISE 5.1

Planning can assist individuals as well as organizations in pursuing goals. Using Cole's activities to assist in good planning:

Establish a career or life goal that you would realistically like to achieve within the next year.

Consider your current situation with regard to reaching this goal. Is it going to be hard, moderate or easy? Are you in a position where achievement of the goal is possible given the resources you have access to? Consider how you will feel once it is achieved.

Identify the resources you may need. These will usually include such things as people, skills, money, opportunity, family situation, attitude, personal strengths or shortcomings, time, and commitment.

Develop a sequence of activities, with targets and timeframes. Be sure you can check off an action or activity every month in order to reinforce your commitment to progress toward the goal. Make sure you monitor your progress and are strict with yourself.

Why Planning Is Not Always Done

Often planning is not done and decisions are made without having gone through any formal planning. There may be many reasons for this, including:

- inability to set goals
- resistance to change
- time constraints
- qualitative measures
- unforeseen changes.

Inability to Set Goals

A manager's inability to set goals may be due to:

- lack of confidence in performing the planning process
- lack of training and understanding of the need to plan
- lack of organizational or environmental knowledge, making it difficult to plan
- fear of failure that is far more apparent when a written plan has been devised and progress assessed against it.

Resistance to Change

Planning for change, unless it involves those affected and has been widely communicated and discussed, can be threatening for many staff. There may be resistance to change due to a variety of factors including:

- staff with low morale or self-esteem
- vested interests happy with the status quo
- staff concerned over a loss of skills or seniority based on experience.

Time Constraints

The time taken to prepare any complex, longer-term plan, particularly involving staff consultation, will be significant. This may inhibit busy managers, limiting the level of planning undertaken.

Qualitative Measures

It is more difficult to account for qualitative (rather than just quantitative) measures in any plan. It is easy to specify the number of newspaper pages that are expected to be digitized in the coming year and then to compare that number with the number actually digitized. However, it is far more difficult to assess the quality (primarily readability) of the end result.

Unforeseen Changes

Concern that longer-term plans will not be able to take into account unforeseen changes, particularly in rapidly developing areas such as changes in technology and online services, can lead to their being discredited. It is essential that these plans allow for change and be flexible enough to take advantage of new developments.

Planning in Nonprofit Organizations

Some issues are particularly relevant to organizations such as libraries and information centers where the bottom line is not to make a clearly identifiable profit, but to provide a quality service that shows good use of the funding received. Some of these issues are:

- the diversity of services provided – how do you compare between them?
- the difficulty of preparing or stockpiling a 'ready-made product' to meet anticipated demand
- the difficulty in many areas of evaluating the quality of service provided and user satisfaction
- the difficulty of costing out services accurately
- the lack of a mass-produced product, and the individuality of the service provided
- reliance upon individual skills to provide service quality.

CHAPTER FIVE   Planning   49

Issues such as these complicate the planning process and make it more difficult to evaluate success or failure of the plan when reviewing progress. However, the fact that the process may be more difficult and time consuming and less specific in its measurable outcomes does not mean that it should not be undertaken!

EXERCISE 5.2

As the manager of a media monitoring service employing a large number of contract employees who work from home, Patrick has decided to update the data gathering system to keep track of all the work being done, who does the work, and payments to employees. Under each of the headings provided, consider some of the factors that may make Patrick reluctant to draw up a detailed plan for implementing the new system.

Inability to set goals

Resistance to change

Time constraints

Qualitative measures

Unforeseen changes

SCENARIO

In a small group, consider the following case study as if you were the manager or supervisor. Use the discussion in this chapter as a guide and brainstorm other ideas and options. You are expected to deliver a practical and workable solution that is in the best interests of the staff and the organization.

"This whole inventory business has been a complete mess and waste of time," muttered Nada in exasperation. She thought back on what she had wanted to achieve at the end of last semester. With the new library management system up and running, Nada had thought it would be a simple matter to undertake an inventory and come out with a clear understanding of what was missing, what was on loan, what had been mis-shelved, and total holdings for various areas of the collection.

Instead, the end result was a mess, and Nada had no confidence in what the system was telling her. Sadly, she realized she should have planned the exercise in far more detail.

Consider the issues Nada needed to plan for in conducting this inventory and how it could have been done better, using Cole's six basic planning steps as a guide.

References and Further Reading

Cole, Kris, *Management: theory and practice,* 3rd edition. Sydney, Pearson, 2005.

Holley, R.P., 'Library planning and budgeting: a few underappreciated principles', *Journal of Library Administration* 54:8, 2014.

Hyman, S.C., 'Planning and creating a Library Learning Commons', *Teacher Librarian* 41:3, 2014.

King, Julie, *Writing an effective business plan*, [online]. www.canadaone.com/ezine/nov00/business_plan1.html

Mittenthal, Richard A., *Ten keys to successful strategic planning for non profit and foundation leaders*, [online], 2002. http://www.tccgrp.com/pdfs/per_brief_tenkeys.pdf

Somerville, M.M. & L. Collins, 'Collaborative design: a learner-centered library planning approach', *The Electronic Library* 26:6, 2008.

Wejrowski, K. & M. McRae, 'Developing a culture of readers through effective library planning', *Knowledge Quest* 42:1, 2013.

CHAPTER SIX
Strategic Planning

Introduction

Strategic planning is concerned with the long-term direction of an organization. It deals with issues such as defining mission statements, analyzing environments, considering alternatives, and selecting a path to pursue. It is a continuing, systematic process for any organization, forming part of an endless cycle that usually involves staff at all levels in planning, decision-making, teamwork, and evaluation.

Strategic planning provides the framework within which operational plans, concerned with the day-to-day running of the organization, are developed. Above strategic planning lies the mission or vision statement, outlining in very broad terms the business of the organization and where it is heading.

Mission Statement

The mission statement is intended to provide a high-level description of the purpose of an organization. Usually it is a concise paragraph or two dealing with the fundamental reasons for the organization's existence. It lays down in extremely broad terms the overall aims or purpose of the organization. While these will inevitably change, there is usually an underlying continuity about the mission.

It is important that staff members understand the mission statement and relate to its goals, which they must feel are meaningful and achievable. Customers and stakeholders should also understand the purpose of the organization as expressed in its mission statement.

 As defined on its website,

> *"The mission of the University of Toronto Library is to foster the search for knowledge and understanding in the University and the wider community. To this end, we shall provide innovative services and comprehensive access to information founded upon our developing resources as one of the leading research libraries in the world."*

This statement succinctly expresses the university's overall purpose, without attempting to define how its mission is to be carried out, and is followed by a 'Statement of Service Values' that guide it. These values provide the underlying principles upon which all of the activities undertaken to achieve this mission should be based. These are important as not only setting parameters within which all work is undertaken but also in providing a very public statement on the core philosophy of the Library.

Similarly, in developing its strategic direction to 2020, the British Library describes its vision (which can also be seen as its medium term mission) as:

"In 2020, the British Library will be a leading hub in the global information network, advancing knowledge through our collections, expertise and partnerships, for the benefit of the economy and society and the enrichment of cultural life."

In one sentence the British Library outlines its aims and philosophy for the foreseeable future. In addition, it talks of its global role (not just the United Kingdom), its collections and expertise, and its desire to collaborate via partnerships in order to benefit both the economy and cultural life, both important factors in ensuring its relevance in the 21st century.

Strategic Planning

Supporting the mission are strategic plans or initiatives that focus the organization's direction in achieving its mission. These are long-term strategies, yet are regularly reviewed to ensure their relevance and appropriateness in a rapidly changing environment. The strategies adopted will support broader organizational aims that may concentrate on growth or expansion, stability, and maintenance of market share, or possibly downsizing and retrenchment.

Examples of strategic directions in the library and information industries may be:

- growth industries: e-publishing (both books and serials); online delivery; traditional heritage and preservation; and digital preservation and repositories
- stable industries: traditional printing and publishing; library management systems
- declining industries: microfilm and microfiche technologies; printed encyclopedias and other physical reference works.

The plan is usually developed by senior management who must then communicate it properly throughout the organization in order to ensure broad 'ownership' of its objectives. Focus groups may be used with staff—and frequently customers—to find out more about how the organization is performing, to gain ideas as to where it should be going, and, most importantly, to find out where it is not achieving.

Closely associated with the plan are its related **performance indicators**. These will be devised while the plan is being developed, to act as a measure of success. They are important in any evaluation of the effectiveness of the steps taken in achieving the plan as well as in its actual outcomes.

Make sure the indicators are as 'measurable' as possible and try to avoid purely qualitative measures such as 'improved customer relations', 'a higher profile within the college', etc. Try to devise measures that can be quantified, e.g., by surveying customers before and after a customer-relations program has been put in place, in order to measure whether satisfaction levels have risen. For example, one can set a benchmark—say, 80% of users surveyed will feel that they received a high level of service compared to 50% before the program—by which to measure relative success or failure.

EXERCISE 6.1

Using the mission statement of the British Library given above, create what you feel may be the strategic plans necessary to achieve the part of their mission statement talking about benefitting the economy and enriching cultural life.

Steps in Developing a Strategic Plan

Once the mission statement has been shaped into a clear statement of overall objectives, the strategic plan can be developed to achieve its goals. This can be time consuming and difficult, but it is essential to provide direction over the medium term. By building suitable control measures into the associated operational plans it should be possible to assess progress toward the strategic objectives.

These basic steps are necessary to develop a strategic plan:

- *Ensure that the mission statement is clear and concise and correctly summarizes the role of the organization.* If the mission relates to a subunit of a larger organization, such as a library within a university, it must fit comfortably within the organization's culture and support the overall mission of the organization. Thus, government departments, schools, and universities will all have broad mission statements that the libraries in these institutions need to support.
- *Evaluate internal and external factors* using devices such as the SWOT analysis (strengths, weaknesses, opportunities, threats) as discussed earlier. Involve staff and users in this analysis in order to gain depth and breadth of input.
- *Evaluate current performance level and availability of resources.* Assess existing strengths and weaknesses. Conduct comparisons with like organizations and learn as much as possible about their strategic plans and concerns.
- *Clearly define the organizational philosophy (this relates to values) that is supported by top management.* This philosophy relates to fundamental issues that define the shape and nature of the service provided. Ensure that no major policies contradict each other, or will hinder achievement of the 'big picture' goals.
- *Consider the values of the organization and how they shape its culture and activities.* These have usually developed over time and will have a big influence on organizational philosophy. Planning needs to use these values as a basis upon which to build, rather than see them as a hindrance to future growth.
- *Determine user demand* by talking to users and nonusers, conducting surveys, and searching the literature. Reassess target groups, market segments, and user needs. Consider future trends.
- Using the information gathered, *develop a set of objectives and priorities focusing on long-term success and growth* for the organization.

Traditionally, strategies and priorities concentrate on providing value for money—e.g., the best product at the lowest competitive price; providing a product clearly different from the competition's; or concentrating upon one market segment or target group. For libraries and information centers, they may include keeping costs down for the parent organization while maintaining a high level of service; providing a valuable information service not easily duplicated by the end-user or outside sources; or building a highly specialized, targeted and comprehensive collection of resources for a topic or area.

Remember that strategic planning is a continuous process that involves:
- *evaluating the results of earlier planning,*
- *amending plans in light of changes in the environment, user needs, or other causes,*
- *remaining flexible enough to grasp new opportunities and avoid unforeseen pitfalls.*

Strategic Planning—Why and Why Not?

Strategic planning does have its critics and, quite frequently, is not done to the depth and degree necessary to provide a solid base for future growth. Like all activities, there are benefits and costs to strategic planning. It is important to consider both when deciding on the extent to which the organization will devote resources to it.

Benefits

The benefits of strategic planning vary across organizations, depending on the nature of their businesses and the environments within which they operate. Generally, however, strategic planning will:

- motivate the management team
- force management to consider its key objectives
- provide a framework for operational planning and help keep it on track
- act as a control against management going off on 'hare-brained' schemes
- help maintain focus during periods of rapid change
- stimulate awareness of strategic issues among management and staff
- contribute to innovation
- increase staff awareness of the business environment
- promote better coordination of activities and resource allocation
- provide staff with a vision for the future
- help promote the organization to external groups such as funding bodies.

As well as benefits, of course, there are costs.

Costs

The problems inherent in strategic planning sometimes cause it to fall out of favor as a management tool. Most of these difficulties lie outside the organization's control, leading to frustration when carefully laid plans cannot be pursued. Problems include:

- the difficulty of planning medium- to long-term in a rapidly changing environment that can be quite unpredictable
- the volume of information required to devise the plan
- the time taken to produce the plan
- the need for flexibility to meet unforeseen challenges and opportunities, and not to be tied down to a plan drawn up months before
- the lack of support from staff more usually concerned with short-term, even day-to-day activities
- lack of understanding of, or support for, strategic planning within the parent organization
- the possibility that resources may not be available when it is time to implement the plan
- unrealistic, impractical plans that do not match organizational resources, values, or philosophy.

Many of these problems can be addressed in the early stages of working on strategic issues. Some may seem insurmountable in a particular situation (e.g., if you are a farmer, it is impossible to control the weather). However, it is often possible to build processes into the operational plans supporting the strategy to help deal with such problems (e.g., the farmer can take out insurance). While strategic planning does come in and out of favor, it is generally seen as central to management activity.

 EXERCISE 6.2

Despite fierce competition and high attrition among ebook vendors, the new Consort Ebook Agency hopes to be a pioneer in the emerging market for ebook subscriptions based on usage offering attractive, flexible licensing plans to consortia and their member libraries.

Devise a mission statement that may be appropriate for the Consort Ebook Agency.

Produce three strategies related to achieving the mission of the agency.

SCENARIO

In a small group, consider the following case study as if you were the manager or supervisor. Use the discussion in this chapter as a guide and brainstorm other ideas and options. You are expected to deliver a practical and workable solution that is in the best interests of the staff and the organization.

A government entity has the following mission statement:

"The Australian Bureau of Meteorology's mission is to provide Australians with environmental intelligence for safety, sustainability, security, well-being and prosperity."

Brian is the manager of a special library within the department.

Devise a mission statement for the library in support of the Bureau's mission.

Consider why Brian might have some difficulty in developing strategic plans for his library.

📖 References and Further Reading

Australia. Bureau of Meteorology, *Strategic Plan 2015-2020*, [online]. http://www.bom.gov.au/info/leaflets/strategic-plan-2015-20.pdf

British Library, *Our mission and 2020 vision*, [online]. http://www.bl.uk/aboutus/stratpolprog/2020vision/themes/

Casey, A.M., 'Grassroots strategic planning: involving library staff from the beginning', *Journal of Library Administration* 55:4, 2015.

Ladwig, J. Packer, 'Assess the state of your strategic plan', *Library Administration and Management* 19:2, Spring 2005.

Matthews, Stephen A. & Kimberly D. Matthews, *Crash course in strategic planning*. Santa Barbara, CA., Libraries Unlimited, 2013.

New York University Libraries, *Strategic plan 2013-2017*, [online]. http://library.nyu.edu/about/Strategic_Plan.pdf

University of Toronto, *Mission statement*, [online]. https://onesearch.library.utoronto.ca/mission-statement

Wade, M., 'Re-inventing the library: the role of strategic planning, marketing and external relations, and shared services at the National Library of Scotland', *Library Review* 62:1/2, 2013.

Wayne, Richard, 'The academic library strategic planning puzzle: putting the pieces together', *College & Research Libraries News* 72:1, 2012. http://crln.acrl.org/content/72/1/12.full

CHAPTER SEVEN
Operational Planning

Introduction

Operational planning occurs at the bottom level of the planning hierarchy and is concerned with setting out the short-term programs and activities necessary to make progress toward long-term objectives detailed in the strategic plan. Involving both front-line and middle management, operational planning concerns inputs and outputs, resources and constraints, and how these can be managed to meet strategic objectives.

Operational plans are for the shorter term, providing the means to implement the longer-term strategy. These plans give life to the overall strategy by spelling out very specific activities to achieve the broader goals announced in the strategic plan. It is through these plans and their related performance indicators that progress toward broader aims can be measured. Thus, it is suggested operational plans must be:

- Specific
- Measurable
- Attainable
- Relevant
- Time constrained.

Always remember that operational plans should tie in directly with the broader, strategic goals of the organization.

It is one of the major roles of supervisors or front-line management to provide these operational plans using the management functions described earlier:

- to organize the human, financial, and other resources needed to undertake the task
- to direct, lead, and motivate in achieving the task
- to measure and control activity against the plan.

 Keep in mind that in devising operational plans it is vital to include the staff members who are expected to implement them.

Not only does this provide an opportunity for staff to be involved and understand organizational goals; it has also been shown to boost staff commitment to the goals they have helped to establish. Staff will also have a good idea of what can or cannot be achieved, will provide pragmatic input into setting realistic timeframes, and are likely to have experience and knowledge of the effort and resources required.

It is incumbent on supervisors and managers to involve staff in operational planning; but final decisions rest with management, who must then explain clearly the reasons why a certain course of action is to be adopted, particularly if it was not the approach favored by staff.

As an example of how the levels of planning relate, consider the mission of a hypothetical public library:

> "To provide educational and recreational resources to the residents of its county in a cost-effective manner, to act as a repository of local history, and to offer access to information resources held outside the local area."

In support of this mission, one of the library's strategic plans may be to ascertain whether or not the purchasing program for adult fiction is meeting the recreational needs of residents.

The operational plans necessary to implement the strategic plan will include designing and conducting surveys of users and nonusers of the collection; measuring collection usage; reviewing selection policy; and so on.

Designing Operational Plans

Stoner (1992, p. 254) discusses a number of basic steps in general decision-making that can readily be applied to the introduction of new strategies, whether an organization is product or service–oriented. These steps are still relevant today, providing a sound checklist of issues to consider when developing operational plans to achieve these higher level strategies. Operational plans range from simple procedures—like dealing with an increase in the number of reference questions in a special library—to more complex activities such as a change in the computer system. Regardless of the level of complexity involved, it is useful to consider the following aspects of any proposal:

- research and investigation
- developing alternatives
- evaluation and selection
- implementation.

Research and Investigation

Research and investigation is necessary to understand all the issues involved, to clarify the nature of the problem being addressed, and to determine the objectives desired from the plan. It will also help answer questions such as 'what are the critical aspects?' and 'where might the pressure points be?'

Depending on the objective to be achieved (which will affect the complexity and impact of the plan), this research phase should usually involve staff at all levels and be the first step in building their commitment to the plan's implementation.

Alternatives

The design of any new service or product or the upgrading of existing procedures should emphasize quality, reliability and cost-effectiveness. As a general principle, keep it simple. Staff members have to be trained in new practices and procedures; customers may have to get used to new systems; and management may have to accept a short-term loss of productivity during the implementation or changeover phase. Aim to identify as many practical alternatives as possible and be careful not to jump at the first option that seems to meet your needs.

Staff should be involved in the search for alternative approaches if it will affect the way they do things, and this is a good opportunity to encourage creativity and engage them in brainstorming solutions.

Evaluation and Selection

Choice of appropriate action is based on a balance of the resources available and the objectives to be achieved. The 'perfect' solution may not be adopted for any number of reasons. If not, it will be important that staff and senior management be made aware of why compromises have been made and a less-than-perfect solution implemented.

Always ensure when deciding on the course of action that broader organizational philosophy and strategies are supported. Thus, before setting in place any changes, be sure to consider their impact on:

- staff
- customers
- the organization.

Finally, note any risks or uncertainties associated with the chosen approach and make sure these are carefully noted for follow-up in the implementation stage.

Implementation

The following should also be considered when bringing in a new or changed system:

- *Staff should be involved at all stages* from planning to implementation. For simple activities that have little impact on the work flow, involvement may simply mean a discussion during a coffee break. For more major decisions, formal meetings, budgets and schedules will be necessary, covering all aspects of the proposed change.
- *Think about technology and the role it will play in the new process*. Whatever activity is planned, in the library and information professions there will probably be some reliance on technology. This may prompt concerns relating to training in that particular package; and availability, reliability, and capability of equipment. Depending on the nature of the plan, it may be necessary to consider such questions as the following: What will happen if the system goes down? How will slow response time affect the work? What if there are no network outlets on this side of the office?
- *The design of the work flows associated with the plan needs careful thought* to ensure the best possible outcome. There may be occupational safety and health issues to be considered, levels of job satisfaction to be maintained or improved, and relationships within the department or externally to be taken into account. There may also be individual concerns of staff affected by the plan. Do they feel capable of implementing it? By making previous practices obsolete does it require that they master new skills? Is their performance more readily assessable under the new system? These individual concerns have to be appreciated and dealt with by the manager responsible for implementing new procedures.
- *Training is a major issue that may need to be planned and budgeted for* in the implementation of new activities or major upgrading of old ones. Staff should feel that they will be capable of performing the new tasks effectively. The level of training required will range from a simple question-and-answer session in the work environment for a minor change of procedure (e.g., a new booking form for audio-

visual equipment in a school library) to formal off-the-job training in order to implement a new library management system.

- *Some form of performance and monitoring measures need to be in place* to gauge the success of any new plan. Depending on what is being undertaken, it may include measures of quality, output, cost, timeliness, customer satisfaction, level of backlog, etc. These measures need to be carefully thought out beforehand, with all staff understanding how the new work practices will be assessed. Staff should also be clear on the timeframe needed for the new system to get up to speed.

 EXERCISE 7.1

Nikhil works for the customer hotline at the state internal revenue service. His main job is to answer questions from the public about what is and isn't tax deductible. In the past, his work often involved considerable time with individual callers, going through the tax code, finding additional information, etc.

Due to staff cuts, the number of hotline staff has been reduced, raising the workload for Nikhil and the others dramatically. Following a directive from the revenue service administration, the hotline manager has been discussing with the staff the implementation of a new system. In this system, callers would be told that if their question takes longer than five minutes to answer, they will have to decide whether to pay a fee of $50 per hour (minimum charge $25) for a staff member to continue with their problem, or to go to a private accountant.

Nikhil is concerned about this change, despite having been consulted about its possible adoption. Using the headings below, what are some of the issues that may be of concern to Nikhil?

His involvement in the decision and its implementation

The new or changed technology requirements

Training requirements

The impact on work flows

Performance assessment

Planning Tools

A number of techniques and procedures have been developed to help managers formulate plans and oversee their implementation. The main aim of these techniques is to enable managers to schedule activities and resources properly, so that they can proceed in the right order and be available as required. These techniques can also be useful as a pilot study to assess the feasibility of projects, particularly those that are more complex, before full-scale application.

These planning tools, and many others, are available as free open source software or more sophisticated, purchased packages that enable complex planning to be undertaken rapidly and simply. Updating or changing is easy, and so is emailing or printing out copies of the plan for interested parties. However, for simpler projects, manual methods using paper and pencil are still appropriate and very useful.

We will look at examples of these techniques:
- Gantt chart
- PERT network
- modeling.

Gantt Chart

The Gantt chart is a well-known graphical means for planning the progress of an activity. Usually, activities are listed along the vertical axis while the horizontal axis represents a time line. Activities are listed in the order in which they need to happen and a line is drawn along the chart to represent when they should start and end. The chart makes evident potential clashes or overlaps, the amount of time each activity will take, and how a project is progressing.

The example below illustrates how the chart can be used to plan production of a new 'Guide to Special Collections' in a large library, to be added to the library's web page and to be available as a printed pamphlet within the library.

Activity	1	2	3	4	5	6	7	8	9	10	11	12
Decide on scope of the guide	****											
Determine staff and other resource requirements		*****										
Liaise with website manager and design of guide (web and print)		*****										
Write proposal, gain administrative approval			*****									
Research, collate information				*************								
Enter into publishing package					**************							
Digitize images to include in the Guide					*********							
Design cover, page layout (for print) and web design and links for online					************							
Edit, review content								******				
Compile sample copy for sign off									******			
Upload to website											****	
Print copies and distribute											****	

The chart shows how long each activity is supposed to take, those tasks that are concurrent, and those that must follow in sequence. As tasks are completed, the chart can be updated with a line that shows the actual time taken. This acts as a measure of control indicating to the manager how well the project is keeping to schedule and how delays may push out the completion date.

PERT Network

The Program Evaluation and Review Technique (PERT)—also known as critical path analysis—is more sophisticated than the Gantt chart. It is used in planning more complex projects, usually through a computer software package, which adds greatly to its flexibility and ease of use. Essentially, it has the same aims as the Gantt chart—to assist with scheduling and assess progress—but is more able to highlight potential bottlenecks. The simple example below illustrates how it might be used to plan the installation of a mobile compact shelving unit in an area previously occupied by stationary shelving.

Activity		Expected Time (days)	Prerequisite Activity
A	Measure floor area	1	None
B	Check floor loading and levelness	1	None
C	Order appropriate compact shelving	1	A, B
D	Advise users of disruption	1	None
E	Pack up materials	3	D
F	Dismantle, remove old shelves	1	E
G	Level floor	5	F
H	Install compact shelving	2	C, G
I	Move materials into compact shelving	2	H

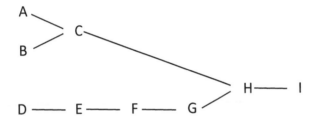

From this network diagram it is easy to see how long the job will take, where concurrent activities can be undertaken, and where problems may occur.

Modeling

Modeling or simulation may be used to test plans before they are implemented in practice. It is particularly useful for testing options that involve the use of various combinations of materials.

Testing can be done manually or using computer software.

eg   To plan for, say, the move of a whole office to another building, modeling may take the form of a diagram of the new office area, using paper cutouts of workstations, desks, bookcases, etc. Thus arrangement of the furniture in the new area can be worked out before the move, reducing the difficulty and time involved in moving. Only a pencil, ruler, paper, scissors, tape, and glue stick are required.

More sophisticated modeling could be undertaken using room design software that allows users to view floor plans from various angles and to manipulate the components being moved, in order to make the best possible use of the space available.

All these approaches are relatively simple to use, offering an easy, yet useful, method of successful project planning.

EXERCISE 7.2

Construct a Gantt chart that shows the steps and approximate times involved in relocating a college library from its current premises to a new building 50 yards away across a parking lot.

SCENARIO

In a small group, consider the following case study as if you were the manager or supervisor. Use the discussion in this chapter as a guide and brainstorm other ideas and options. You are expected to deliver a practical and workable solution that is in the best interests of the staff and the organization.

As a cataloging supervisor Scott is aware of a package of over 200 individual pieces of sheet music that have just been acquired by the library. His director is particularly interested in this collection and has asked for it to be 'processed' as quickly as possible. Neither Scott nor any of his staff have experience handling sheet music.

In his initial research of the problem, what are some of the issues Scott will need to foresee and what planning will be required to help overcome them? Use the points below as a guide:

Physical processing (labeling, shelving, etc.)

Cataloging (level, standards, copy cataloging, etc.)

Staff training

Impact on other work

📖 References and Further Reading

Chester County Library System, *2014-2016 transitional operational plan,* [online], 2014.
http://www.ccls.org/assets/pdfs/2014-2016CCLSTransitionalPlanApproved12114.pdf

Crumpton, M.A., 'Building operational efficiencies', *The Bottom Line* 26:1, 2013.

Duggan, Tara, *Using tools and techniques to optimize project outcomes,* [online], 2011.
http://www.brighthubpm.com/software-reviews-tips/125683-using-scheduling-tools-and-
techniques-to-optimize-project-outcomes/

Hennen, Thomas, *Hennen's public library planner: a manual and interactive CD-ROM*, New
York, Neal-Schuman, 2004. Introduction available at:
http://www.haplr-index.com/nshennen_fm.pdf

Jeal, Yvette, 'Strategic alignment at the University of Manchester Library: ambitions,
transitions, and new values', *New Review of Academic Librarianship* 20:3, 2014.

Leoisaac.com. *Additional components of an operational plan,* [online].
http://www.leoisaac.com/operations/top211.htm

Massis, B.E., 'Project management in the library', *New Library World* 111:11/12, 2010.

Stoner, James A. F. and R. Edward Freeman, *Management,* 5th ed., Englewood Cliffs, N.J.,
Prentice-Hall, 1992.

CHAPTER EIGHT
Event Planning

Introduction

One type of planning that many library and information center managers may be required to do is for special events. It could be the launch of a book week or a readathon; the visit of a celebrity such as an author; a politician opening an extension; or a conference, workshop, or seminar.

All these events will benefit from careful planning following the steps discussed in earlier chapters. It is also useful to consider in detail some specific points related to organizing events. Depending upon the size and nature of the event, some or all of the activities discussed in this chapter will need to be undertaken. Obviously, the bigger and more complex an event, the more care needs to be taken in addressing these issues.

Planners should be sure to do each of the following:
- establish clear and prioritized goals for the event
- if appropriate, spell out a theme, slogan, and logo to tie activities together
- be clear about the target audience
- sell the event to your staff and superiors
- prepare a schedule of activities covering the planning, the event itself, and its follow-up
- decide on guests, activities, levels of catering, location, etc.
- draw up a budget as early as possible
- allocate staff and other resources to the event
- market the event—publicity, promotion, social media platforms etc.
- conduct the event
- follow up and evaluate.

Goals and Priorities

Explicit goals are crucial to the success of any enterprise. Is an 'MS Readathon' campaign just to raise money for multiple sclerosis research, or does it have other goals such as encouraging reading in young people, greater use of the library collection, improved literacy skills, raised awareness of multiple sclerosis, etc.? Usually events have a range of goals within one major objective. It pays to be clear about these goals, including defining the target audience (e.g., 6- to 12-year-olds, the department's senior management, etc.). Spell them out and prioritize them.

Once this work has been done it is easier to plan the next steps: the type of event, whether linking with other groups will be necessary, proposed audience and activities, costs, timing, and duration. Then it may also be possible to devise a catchy slogan or logo with which to lead a promotional campaign and spark interest among the target audience. Also, with the goals clearly spelled out, it is easier for senior management to be clear on what it is endorsing and, once it is over, to evaluate how successful the event has been.

Selling the Event

In order to 'sell' the event, you need to build enthusiasm and support among staff as well as senior management. Doing so is not always easy, since the event will no doubt impose additional work on already busy people. Make sure that staff are involved as much as possible from the start and discuss their concerns openly. Something else may have to take a lower priority over this period. In that case, be explicit about it so that it is clear to everyone.

When presenting the case to senior management, point out if other activities may suffer so that management will not be taken by surprise if other things slide. Management needs this information to help it assess the priority of this or any new activity.

Scheduling

If the event has any degree of complexity, a clear, detailed timetable needs to be drawn up covering the planning period, the activity, and the aftermath. Scheduling can never be too early. A good schedule helps immeasurably to reduce the stress of event preparation. A sample schedule for a moderate-sized conference is given later in this chapter.

Activities, Guests, etc.

The activities involved, the question of guests, and the style and location of the action all depend upon the nature of the event. Thus a readathon, conducted by the local library, would require very little in the way of location or activity planning, although a guest speaker to address parents' or seniors' clubs may be appropriate.

Guests are an attractive option in many ways but require careful planning to ensure a pleasant experience for all parties. They must be met, escorted, have a decent-sized audience, and may require security (if politicians or celebrities). They should give a speech of appropriate length, and may need to have their costs (e.g., travel) refunded.

Location, if outside the normal facilities, requires additional work. If outside, there are concerns about the weather, parking, permission to use the site, seating, toilet facilities, catering, security, etc. These concerns are relevant anywhere, but become particularly acute outdoors. If indoors in an unusual location, be sure that the space is adequate, that you have the necessary keys, that rest rooms are nearby and adequate for the expected numbers, and that Wi-Fi access is available for everyone.

Budgets

Once the broad aims of the event have been decided, a budget estimate can be determined. It will be used to give senior management a general idea of the cost of the event in relation to its size and scope. Management will then be able to judge whether or not the activity can be funded and whether the proposed cost seems reasonable. Once line management has given an in-principle go-ahead, planning of location, activities, etc. will generate a more detailed and accurate budget. Then senior management can give final approval (or not) for the event to take place.

Staffing and Resources

Remember that staff members will be taking on this work in addition to their normal routine. Involve as many staff as practical, ideally using available talents or expertise, but do make sure that someone has clear accountability for the outcomes. Give people plenty of time and do not hand out 'last minute' jobs. Use external help as necessary and for key roles, making sure that a backup person is designated.

Planning for almost any event will take more time than you first anticipate. Do not underestimate the size of the task and its complexities. Follow the plan carefully, referring regularly to the schedule, and take immediate action if things appear to be slipping—it is easier to fix them now than to leave them and hope they will get sorted out as time passes.

Marketing and Promotion

This is essential to any successful activity. Develop a consistent image (this is where logos, slogans, etc., are useful) and be clear on what is being promoted. Consider a press kit for local media detailing the event, containing invitations to the opening and contact numbers for more information, interviews, etc. Make use of 'free' promotion, e.g., social media (blogs, Facebook, web pages, listservs etc.); interviews with local radio; posters designed by students; talks to local groups, etc.

Conducting the Event

With good planning and preparation, the event will go smoothly. The day before, make sure that you check all aspects of the venue and activities. Consider whether signage is in place to direct visitors. Are guests prepared and still coming? Has the media been informed? Is the mobile phone charged? Do you have cash on hand for emergencies? Have you put off other activities to concentrate on the event? Depending on the size of the function, this preplanning the day before should help to minimize the nasty surprises that can create stress on the day.

Follow-Up

At the end of the function, thank everyone and sort out any financial transactions (before you forget). In the next few days, prepare a follow-up report that examines how well the original goals were met, the costs involved, the difficulties encountered, what worked and what did not. Write and thank invited guests and anyone who put in particular effort. Present your report to management and, if necessary, arrange for auditing the finances. Don't forget to sign off on blogs or Facebook and if appropriate update the conference web pages with proceedings, outcomes etc.

EXERCISE 8.1

Katrina and three other staff run a medium-sized secondary school library. They are planning to raise awareness of local environmental issues within their school community and to present information about environmental organizations such as the Sierra Club, the Nature Conservancy, and Environmental Defense (Environmental Defence in Canada). Katrina is thinking over this idea and wants to make some notes under the following headings to help in getting the project off the ground.

Clear goals of the proposal

Possible types of events and associated activities

Financial considerations

Publicity and promotion

Scheduling Example

The nature and extent of any schedule is determined by the complexity of the event. However, managers of even simple activities benefit from a clear schedule of tasks to reduce the stress involved in planning and implementation. The following is a suggested schedule for a fairly complex event—organizing a seminar, conference, or workshop that will involve high-profile guests, a venue, promotion, etc.

10-18 months prior	Gain general approval; establish a committee; decide purpose, goals, and audience; set dates; investigate and book venue; brainstorm logo, theme; identify and invite major participants; seek funding and sponsorship. *Committee meets irregularly—say monthly.*
9 months prior	Organize letterhead, stationery, initial mailings; establish web site, blogs and other social media presence; identify relevant listservs and send out early 'hold the date' announcements; seek local support; prepare detailed budget; open bank account; develop a draft program; outline fall back options; check any security or permit issues. *Committee meets twice monthly from now on.*
6 months prior	Detailed emailing to target audience with preliminary program; call for registrations; follow up sponsorship; investigate catering or accommodation for guests; confirm VIPs; confirm audiovisual (AV) and Wi-Fi access in venue; consider props, displays, packets for attendees, etc.
3 months prior	Start publicity, promotion (remembering sponsors); confirm program and update website as program firms up; chase up papers and presentations from presenters and copyright clearance forms; liaise with senior management over the impact on current work; send follow-up mailings and call for registrations; confirm general catering arrangements.
1 month prior	Confirm all participants; contact local radio, press; purchase gifts, name tags, etc.; appoint escorts for VIP guests; send final follow-up to all presenters who have not yet delivered their papers or presentations and to registrants with final details; schedule printing and/or uploading to website as required; arrange media, photographer as necessary; run through backup arrangements. *Committee to meet as required.*
2 weeks prior	Check venue and equipment to be used; meet with critical others— e.g., caterer, computer/AV technician, security, parking; assign tasks to individuals; media blitz.

1 week prior	Give final numbers to caterers; continue media promotion; prepare signs, name tags, maps, etc.; ensure all displays are in place; ensure VIP guest escorts are organized; refresh backup arrangements; make sure your normal job is covered for the crucial period.
1 day prior	Get keys; set up tables, chairs, computer systems etc.; check that VIPs are on schedule and escorts ready; confirm photographer; install signs.
On the day	Be at venue early. Have emergency contact numbers handy, mobile phone available, and someone who can act as a 'runner' to assist. Have receipt book and the ability to take registrations or payments on the day. Make sure a car is available.
1 day after	Clean up venue, return keys. Thank everyone. See that VIPs are happy. Finalize financial transactions.
1-2 weeks after	Update website with papers as appropriate. *Committee reconvenes to evaluate the experience.* Highlight successes and failures—investigate both. Write a report and gather all papers for future events. Arrange auditing if necessary, and thank everyone.

EXERCISE 8.1

Adrian is a librarian involved in planning a major event at the state/provincial or territorial library where he works, to celebrate the opening of a new wing. It will involve book readings from high-profile authors, poetry workshops and seminars, a speech by the governor, and a jazz concert featuring a local band that will attract a large audience. As Adrian is a fan of this particular band, he has been given the task of organizing arrangements at the library once they arrive. What issues will Adrian have to handle?

SCENARIO

In a small group, consider the following case study as if you were the manager or supervisor. Use the discussion in this chapter as a guide and brainstorm other ideas and options. You are expected to deliver a practical and workable solution that is in the best interests of the staff and the organization.

As president-elect of the Association of College and Research Libraries, a division of the American Library Association, Mary is responsible for planning the ACRL President's Program at the ALA Annual Conference in two years. At least 300 people will attend and, as this is the last conference she will attend as president, Mary would really like this program to be very successful and perhaps a little different.

Develop clear goals for the program and then an approximate schedule indicating what (in some detail) will need to be done and when.

References and Further Reading

Comm, Joel, *The quick social media guide to event planning*, [online], 2014.
https://www.salesforce.com/blog/2014/04/social-media-event-planning-gp.html

Dowd, Nancy, 'Social media: libraries are posting but is anyone listening?', *Library Journal* May 7, 2013.

Friedmann, Susan, *Meeting and event planning for dummies*, Hoboken, N.J., Wiley, 2003.

Houston Public Library, *Library events*, [online], 2015.
http://houstonlibrary.org/learn-explore/library-events

Kennedy, J., 'How to plan a special event to promote the library', *Journal of Hospital Librarianship* 11:3, 2011.

Khan, Z. & S.L. Jarvenpaa, 'Exploring temporal coordination of events with Facebook.com', *Journal of Information Technology* 25:2, 2010.

Kroski, Ellyssa, *10 social media marketing tips for libraries,* [online], 2013.
http://oedb.org/ilibrarian/10-social-media-marketing-tips-for-libraries/

Preddy, L., 'Planning a free book night', *School Library Monthly* 28:8, 2012.

School Library Association (UK), *Book event planning tips*, [online], 2015.
http://www.sla.org.uk/book-event-planning-tips.php

CHAPTER NINE
Government Policies and Their Impact on Managers

Introduction

In the last twenty-five years or so governments around the world, particularly those in the Western democracies, have introduced social legislation to make the workplace more responsive to the needs of employees. Laws have also been enacted to increase the rights of users or consumers of goods and services and to provide basic protection of their interests. In addition, there has been a growing expectation that business and large bureaucracies will be 'good' corporate citizens, contributing positively to the society in which they operate, while showing a high level of corporate responsibility.

Major pieces of legislation that have particular relevance to all managers in libraries and information centers deal with issues such as:

- occupational safety and health / occupational health and safety
- copyright / intellectual property
- equal employment opportunity / human rights
- confidentiality of library records / personal information protection
- freedom of information / access to information and privacy.

Each area of legislation is briefly described below and its practical impact discussed. While every jurisdiction will have its own interpretation as to what is covered in these areas, how the law is enforced and the strategies in place to encourage compliance, it is possible to look at these areas in general terms in order to understand their impact on managers in the workplace.

Occupational Safety and Health (OSH)/Occupational Health and Safety (OHS)

Occupational safety and health legislation has been in place in many areas since the 19th century, but it is only more recently, since the 1970s, that it has become commonplace and relevant to work in areas such as the library and information fields.

For both employer and employee, a safe and healthy working environment should be a priority:

- for employers, days lost through sickness and accidents are costly, with lost productivity and impacts on morale, while workers' compensation insurance premiums directly reflect the number of cases that occur in a given workplace and can rise dramatically if the number of incidents rises only slightly
- for employees, it is clearly in their best interest to avoid injuries and suffering.

The supervisors' or managers' responsibilities in this area relate directly to the provision of a safe workplace and much of the legislation spells out unequivocally the responsibility of front-line management. They must take seriously any issue brought to their attention and deal promptly with any concerns. If it can be addressed right away, the manager or supervisor must give priority to the problem. In more complex cases, action must be taken to bring the problem to the attention of appropriate higher-level management, with all steps clearly noted in writing. Meanwhile the supervisor is responsible for ensuring that staff members are aware of the hazard and that all possible steps have been taken to reduce the risk.

 It cannot be stressed enough that safety and health issues must be taken seriously and dealt with promptly. Failure to do so can result in the supervisor or manager being personally liable for any accident that eventuates.

Managers should also ensure that:
- adequate protective clothing is not only supplied but also worn (e.g., safety boots for those working in a warehouse or similar situation)
- appropriate warning signs are provided in hazardous areas
- proper training and induction is given to all employees
- jobs are designed to minimize the risk of harm to employees (e.g., no one is keyboarding for the entire day every day)
- in general, an atmosphere is created that promotes and supports the establishment and maintenance of a safe work environment.

Managers must also make themselves aware of those safety and health guidelines that pertain to work in their areas. Usually there will be a variety of resources—publications, websites, training, consultations, and partnerships—available to assist employers to make their workplaces safer and to comply with the relevant legislation and associated regulations.

Most work areas are subject to regular inspection by safety and health representatives. In a library or similar environment they will mainly be concerned with issues such as ergonomic furniture, air quality and ventilation, the placement of office machinery (photocopier, printers, etc.), cabling and placement of electrical equipment, hygiene, and first-aid facilities and general housekeeping.

EXERCISE 9.1

Victoria heads a small research team working at a public university. She is concerned that several staff members seem to suffer from high levels of stress associated with their work. She feels that this may be due in part to the cramped conditions in which they are all forced to work while the university is undergoing major reconstruction work.

Note under the following headings what steps Victoria could undertake to ascertain the nature and depth of the problem and what actions she could take to try and alleviate it.

Referring to legislation

Discussing with the team

Evaluating equipment

Evaluating conditions

Copyright/Intellectual Property

Copyright concerns the intellectual property that may lie in a work. It has existed in some form in many countries for hundreds of years and was internationally recognized by the Berne Convention of 1886. Today, most countries have some form of legislation that is aimed at protecting individuals' rights in the intellectual property of a work for a certain time after it was produced.

Copyright protects original literary, musical, dramatic, and artistic works in all formats including print, sound recording, video, digital, etc. The copyright in a work is separate from the work itself and is not related to the physical item. It can be bought and sold as a separate, valuable entity. Note that in some countries the law is still catching up with the technology and may not cover audio-visual productions, television or radio broadcasts or born digital entities, including websites.

 While specific inclusions and copyright terms vary according to the jurisdiction (and sometimes the format of the material), generally copyright in works lasts for between 50–70 years after the death of the creator.

The following are of particular concern to libraries:
- infringement of the law will occur where a substantial portion of a work is reproduced without permission, although the meaning of 'substantial' may vary depending upon the legislation
- many copyright laws provide provisions of fair use, meaning any copyrighted material may be copied for criticism, comment, news reporting, teaching, scholarship, and research, without breaching the legislation.

Generally, if unsure as to whether something is allowed or not, it is best to obtain permission from the copyright owner before using copyrighted material. In most countries, various organizations represent the interests of publishers and rights holders. These organizations have developed processes to enable speedy responses to requests to use copyrighted material, as well as providing fair-use guidelines that libraries and information agencies may follow.

In summary, copyright is a complex topic for library staff and information managers. Here are just a few aspects specific to the library and information sector:
- in a college or university, copyright compliance may be divided among several departments, including the campus copy center, the bookstore, the computing center, the audiovisual department, and the library
- some institutions, with the advice of legal counsel, have developed and published comprehensive copyright policies that seek to balance the legitimate rights of educators and researchers with those of producers and distributors
- of special concern to the library is the applicability of fair use to recorded works, photocopying, interlibrary loan, and course reserves
- with the advent of born digital materials, copyright has become an even more challenging and rapidly changing area.

Equal Employment Opportunity (EEO)/Human Rights

In recent years, many Western jurisdictions have introduced equal opportunity and human rights legislation that has real impact upon the way managers fulfil their role.

In particular, managers are expected to:
- build a workplace free of discrimination and harassment
- share and promote a commitment to equity and access across all groups
- foster this attitude among their staff
- help meet the special needs that some groups may have, like access to training or development opportunities, changes to the physical design of the workspace, redesign of the work itself, etc.

The general thrust of such legislation is to make the place of employment a fairer one by making discrimination based on the following factors illegal:
- race
- color
- religion
- sex
- national origin
- age
- disability.

EEO applies to obvious practices such as recruitment and promotion, and in more subtle ways to areas such as job design, provision of specialized equipment where necessary, building or workplace design, training, and cultural awareness when dealing with people from different backgrounds.

For managers working with a diverse staff these issues are hugely important. It is an essential part of their job to ensure that not only is the letter of the law complied with but also that staff practice the spirit of the law in promoting fairness in their treatment of others.

While the legislation is aimed primarily at ensuring individuals, no matter their background, are treated equally when it comes to the work place, it provides a benefit to employers as well. By supporting the employment of those from a wide diversity of backgrounds, the resultant mix of staff can bring a diverse range of experiences and knowledge into an organization. This can provide a 'different' viewpoint, and potentially ideas and opportunities for the organization that would not otherwise have occurred.

Most governments provide extensive advice on their websites and via printed material explaining the application of equal opportunity and human rights legislation, how to enact it in your workplace, how to deal with individual situations and dispute resolution.

Confidentiality of Library Records/Personal Information Protection

In the United States and elsewhere, legislation affecting the confidentiality of library records has been enacted. The thrust of this legislation is to protect the rights of individuals by ensuring that unauthorized persons be denied access to information about what library materials are being using by whom, and by requiring that law enforcement agencies follow strict procedures before being given access to this information.

In particular, the *USA Patriot Act of 2001* gives federal law enforcement agencies broad powers to examine library records, records of bookstore purchases, the contents of computer drives, and other personal records, in order to gather information about possible criminal terrorist activity. In addition, libraries and other agencies are prohibited from making public the fact that they have been subjected to such investigations. However, those organizations whose records are being investigated may seek legal counsel to ensure that laws are being followed.

 It is the manager's duty to ensure that staff members with access to this sort of personal information about staff or clients fully understand their responsibilities under the law and also the need for confidentiality.

Clear policies, procedures, and guidelines should be established to ensure that the provisions of the law are properly implemented and that staff are clear on how to handle personal information and how to process requests to access it. Encourage staff, if they have concerns, to discuss them with their managers.

Related to this is Privacy legislation, something which has become more prominent given the Internet and its ability to make information visible to 'the world'. The nature of the legislation varies across jurisdictions, but in general aims to ensure that "Everyone has the right to respect for his private and family life, his home and his correspondence" (Article 8 of the *European Convention on Human Rights*). For a manager, this means in practice being sensitive with staff issues in particular, making sure personal information that comes to them through their position at work is kept confidential.

Freedom of Information (FOI)/Access to Information (ATI)

Freedom of Information legislation has been commonly adopted across the democratic world. This legislation gives everyone some rights of access to documents concerning them held by government agencies and also rights to access government documents detailing decision-making more broadly. The legislation applies only to government records, and government agencies may refuse to disclose information that would harm national defense or foreign policy, privacy of individuals, proprietary interests of individuals, functioning of government, or other important interests.

Anyone may make an FOI request, provided it is in writing (email is generally acceptable today). Agencies may also require that the requester pay for any cost of duplication and the time spent retrieving the documents requested.

It is important for library or information managers to understand applicable FOI legislation and procedures as they relate to their agencies, and to be prompt in dealing with such requests. In the event of 'unreasonable requests' requiring large amounts of work, the manager should seek clarification from senior management or obtain legal advice on how best to handle the request.

Corporate Responsibility and Governance

'Corporate responsibility' refers to an organization's behavior that is not guided by legislated requirements. Thus while it might be legal to engage in sophisticated tax avoidance schemes, if you are a major international company is it ethical or seen as meeting general societal expectations? For commercial organizations there is a clear imperative to be seen as good corporate citizens giving back to the society that generates your revenue—it makes good business sense to build this positive image of the company.

For libraries and other information agencies, for whom profit is not the major driver, corporate responsibility can be shown in various ways, including:
- reaching out to the potential client base in a warm and welcoming manner
- building the image of the library as the 'third place' (the first being the home, the second the work place)
- playing a key role in their community, whether this be a local government area, school, university, organization etc.

In addition, focusing on practical tactics such as promoting sustainability in building design and use will all help create that positive image of an organization that cares for the wider world, and is not solely focused on itself.

'Corporate governance' refers to how the organization is run. This covers a mix of legislated requirements (e.g., you may have to pay staff legislated minimum wages) but also internal policies, regulations and practices. Again, good governance helps ensure a positive public image for an organization with both staff and the public, building trust and a good reputation with both.

For libraries and information centers, who usually answer to a parent body or board of some sort, ensuring there is a close and harmonious working relationship between the parent body and library management is critical to ensuring the right level of good governance is fostered and the ensuing benefits of a highly positive reputation accrued.

EXERCISE 9.2

As the records manager for a government department, Jan has been asked to develop a set of procedures to be used when handling requests under the Freedom of Information Act in place in her jurisdiction. Using these headings as a guide, consider some of the issues Jan will have to deal with.

Responsibility

Record keeping

Nature of request

Reporting

Charging

SCENARIO

In a small group, consider the following case study as if you were the manager or supervisor. Use the discussion in this chapter as a guide and brainstorm other ideas and options. You are expected to deliver a practical and workable solution that is in the best interests of the staff and the organization.

Christine is a supervisor in the printing and photocopying section of a large university library. For the last few months she has employed an intellectually disabled person, Ken, under a government-supported program where the employer only pays half the salary and the rest is paid by the program.

The arrangement has worked very well. Ken obviously enjoys the work; it has been a good learning experience for the rest of the team in working with a disabled person; and Christine wishes to appoint him permanently to the position (the salary subsidy would continue). However, university recruitment procedures state very clearly that all appointments must be based on merit alone.

Christine is unsure how to proceed: if a position were advertised and a normal interview process conducted, it would be unlikely that any intellectually challenged person could win on merit alone.

Does equal employment opportunity/human rights legislation play a role here? What steps could Christine take in order to make the appointment?

References and Further Reading

The American Library Association, *The USA Patriot Act in the library*, [online], 2015. http://www.ala.org/Template.cfm?Section=ifissues&Template=/ContentManagement/ContentDisplay.cfm&ContentID=32307

Australian Institute of Company Directors, *Good governance principles and guidance for NFP organisations*, [online], 2015. http://www.companydirectors.com.au/goodgovernance

The British Library, *Corporate social responsibility*, [online], 2012. http://www.bl.uk/aboutus/stratpolprog/csr/index.html

Canadian Center for Occupational Health and Safety, *Health and safety guide for libraries*, [online], 2015. http://www.ccohs.ca/products/publications/library_toc.html

Lipinski, Tomas A., ed., *Libraries, museums, and archives: legal issues and ethical challenges in the new information age*, Lanham, Md., Scarecrow Press, 2002.

Skala, Matthew, Brett Bonfield & Mary Fran Torpey, 'Enforcing copyright', *Library Journal* 133:3, Feb 2008.

de Souza, Yvonne, 'Not just data: privacy in the digital age', *Feliciter*, 60:5, 2014. http://www.cla.ca/feliciter/2014/5/PDFs/Feliciter_5_60_Final_Oct.8_14.pdf

Sturges, Paul & Vesna Crnogorac, *The library and Freedom of Information revisited*, [online], IFLA, 2012. http://www.ifla.org/publications/the-library-and-freedom-of-information-revisited

University of Canterbury (New Zealand), *Equal employment opportunity policy*, [online], 2014. www.canterbury.ac.nz/ucpolicy/GetPolicy.aspx?file=Equal-Employment-Opportunity-Policy.pdf

Versoza, Fe Angela, *Occupational safety and health concerns in library work places*, [slideshare presentation - online], 2008. http://www.slideshare.net/verzosaf/occupational-safety-and-health-concerns-in-library-work-places

World Intellectual Property organization (WIPO), *Study on copyright limitations and exceptions for libraries and archives*, [online], 2008. http://www.wipo.int/meetings/en/doc_details.jsp?doc_id=109192

CHAPTER TEN
Human Resource Management

Introduction

Managing people—their recruitment, assessment, mentoring, and guiding—is one of the major tasks that any manager, at any level, must undertake. Often, it is the most time-consuming part of a manager's work and the most demanding. Building effective teams that help the organization reach its goals, while providing opportunities for individuals to achieve their own goals, is every manager's challenge.

Given reduced budgets, rapidly evolving technology, and greater accountability, it has become, more than ever, vital to recruit staff who will be capable of meeting the challenges.

 Note that the American Library Association (ALA) provides for its members a substantial number of guidelines, standards and other resources to assist across the range of human resource management issues.

Recruitment

Successful recruitment lies at the heart of building a strong team. It is extremely important for managers to be directly involved in recruitment and to devise methods and procedures that will, as much as possible, identify the most appropriate candidate for the job.

The complexity and duration of a recruitment search will vary depending upon the rules of the organization and the nature of the position—e.g., a search for someone to fill a clerical position may be advertised locally, involve few people in the process, entail interviews of less than an hour, and be concluded fairly swiftly, whereas a search for an academic librarian with faculty status may be advertised nationally, involve several committees of faculty, staff, and administration in the process, entail interviews of a day or more, and take weeks or months to conclude. Regardless of the position or the process, careful record keeping is essential at all stages.

The following sets forth a 'model' process for conducting and filling a search.

Step 1—Job Description

Before any work can commence on recruiting, the nature of the tasks to be undertaken must be clearly understood. A job description may be developed that breaks the job down into its major and minor functions, or a narrative style of job description may be written that clearly spells out the work required and the way in which it is undertaken.

Developing a job description should not be done in isolation but should involve the direct supervisor of the position, anyone who may already be doing similar work, and, if appropriate to the organization, the union representative. The description should be no longer than one page and should clearly identify the main tasks. Its primary use is to enable potential candidates to understand what they are applying for; it also serves to make the manager think clearly about the work and how it is done, providing an opportunity to identify desirable improvements.

Even if a job description currently exists, managers should spend some time reviewing the description when the position is to be filled in order to think about what is actually required in this job.

Step 2—Skills, Attributes, and Knowledge

With a clear job description, it is possible to consider the skills, knowledge, and attributes necessary for a staff member to do the work well. Criteria should be written against which candidates will be evaluated. These criteria should relate to 'macro' skills or competencies relevant to many positions in the organization (such as teamwork, punctuality, or accuracy) and to more specific position-related skills such as knowledge of metadata and RDA for a cataloging position. Note, however, that it is often difficult to ascertain the level of 'macro' skills possessed by an applicant, unlike technical skills that can usually be measured quite easily.

Step 3—Advertising

Once the job description has been written and the required skills defined, it is possible to go ahead and recruit someone who appears to be suitable.

Recruitment can be done:
- by advertising
- by contacting an employment agency
- via listservs or other web approaches
- or through word of mouth or personal knowledge.

No method is necessarily better than another (although the first two cost money), but many organizations have clear rules and procedures for recruitment, which limit the options available to a manager. If recruitment is to proceed using an informal method (e.g., through the recommendation of a friend), it is still sensible to evaluate the candidate in a formal manner as described below. Many organizations have affirmative action programs requiring that certain positions be advertised in publications aimed at minority groups or women, as well as other media.

Step 4—The Selection Committee

Evaluating candidates inevitably becomes somewhat subjective. However, it is most important to limit this subjectivity as much as possible in order for applicants to be treated fairly, and to get the best person for the job. For this reason, the selection process is generally undertaken by more than one person.

Common practice is to have at least three people comprise a selection (or search) committee:

- one is the chair, often the direct supervisor of the position being filled, although this may vary if the supervisor has little recruitment experience—the role of chair can be demanding, and it is important to have a knowledgeable and experienced person in that position
- the second member should have direct knowledge of the type of work being done, and be able to ask technical questions and to evaluate detailed answers in the interview
- a third person should be drawn from an outside area, say an enthusiastic user of the library or information center, who will view the candidates from a different perspective than the practitioners. Other constituencies may also be represented, depending upon the institution's procedures and the nature of the position.

Note that the committee should comprise both male and female members, to limit subjectivity and to get a wider view of the applicants. Union representation may be appropriate, depending upon local agreements.

Being a member of a selection committee can be a significant undertaking requiring a major commitment of time. All committee members must be aware of this fact and accept that it will add to their normal workload.

Step 5—Applications
With the selection committee in place, applications may be sought in any of the ways noted above. Applicants should be given a copy of the job description and selection criteria, outlining the skills and knowledge required from a person doing the work. They should then apply formally, in writing, describing how they meet the skills and knowledge requirements listed.

Depending upon the organization's policy, applications may be submitted via email or through the use of a web-based form. Usually, they will also include a résumé or a curriculum vitae (CV) listing the applicants' educational and employment history and any other relevant information. As some written expression is needed in virtually any position in the library and information sector, this written application is an important factor in the assessment.

Step 6—Reviewing Applications
The selection committee should then go through the written applications to assess who are the likely candidates to be selected for interview. Even if there is only one applicant, an interview should be undertaken unless the committee knows the applicant. Generally, limit the number of applicants interviewed to a maximum of five or six for one position and eight to ten if two positions are available, unless special circumstances apply.

Advise those not selected for an interview as soon as possible. It is unkind to keep them waiting unduly (although this decision is sometimes in the hands of a separate office and out of the manager's control). If resources are limited and the number of applicants is likely to be large, an institution may include in the job description words to the effect that 'applicants who have not been advised of an interview time within four weeks [say] of the closing date of the advertisement should assume that they have not been selected for an interview'.

Step 7—Interviewing Candidates

There is little direct evidence to suggest that an interview materially assists in selecting the best candidate. However, it is rare that this process is not carried out, and for virtually all situations with more than one candidate, interviews will be held. At the very least, this process will help the selection committee to gain an impression of the candidate's personality (outgoing, quiet, forward-thinking, etc.) and knowledge in certain concrete areas such as legislative requirements, technical understanding, and service ethic. It is unlikely to provide insights into an individual's level of motivation or initiative, coping with stress, or interpersonal skills when dealing with, say, a difficult client.

Assuming that interviews are undertaken, the selection committee should meet beforehand to discuss questions appropriate to the skills and competencies sought and to formalize arrangements regarding note taking, seating arrangements, etc. It is generally a good idea for all members of the committee to take brief notes during the interview to assist in later evaluation.

Step 8—The Interview

The interviews should be scheduled at least one hour apart, with the candidates advised at the beginning of an interview that it is expected to last, say, 40 minutes and comprise ten or however many questions. It is preferable to use a smaller number of probing questions rather than a large number of a kind which can easily be answered. Interviews for certain types of positions, such as librarians with faculty status in a college or university, may last for a day or more and involve meetings with various groups and individuals and possibly a public presentation.

Peace and quiet are important, as is a comfortable environment. It is good practice, after a candidate has been welcomed and introduced, to start the interview with a general question regarding his or her experience in order to set the person at ease. Further questions should include 'hypotheticals' in which a brief case-study scenario is explained and candidates are asked how they would deal with it. Responses to these 'real life' situations are valuable in assessing a candidate's overall ability.

If at all possible, candidates should be asked to handle a practical task related to the position. Always ensure that candidates are advised that this will be a requirement before they arrive for the interview.

 For example,

- for an interlibrary loan position, it is reasonable to expect applicants to undertake some hands-on work using OCLC's WorldShare system
- if written work is important in an information center, completing a précis of a document or writing a memo on a particular subject may be an appropriate task
- if the position involves library cataloging it may be useful to have the applicant create a bibliographic record or amend a downloaded copy cataloging record.

Step 9—Evaluation

Evaluation and ranking of applicants will be undertaken by the selection committee, taking into account the original application, performance at interview, and references (preferably gained through conversation with referees). Oral references are often more useful than written letters of reference. Referees are generally reluctant to state adverse opinions in writing, whereas a conversation allows for a wider discussion of a candidate's strengths and weaknesses. The person who talks with the referee should take careful notes that become part of the selection 'paper trail'.

The most important criteria (and unfortunately the most difficult to assess) relate to intangibles such as motivation, teamwork, positive approach, client focus, etc. These attributes are more difficult to develop than technical skills, which are readily acquired with a reasonable level of training and practice. Thus in assessing candidates and communicating with referees it is useful to focus on these 'soft' skills in order to try and gain a clearer understanding of how the candidate works in a team environment (very few people work on their own) and manage a sometimes busy and stressful workplace.

Step 10—Appointment

Appointment of the successful candidate will follow the procedures laid down in your organization, and an orientation program is vital, together with a probationary period. These are discussed below. Unsuccessful applicants should be advised as soon as possible and offered a personal conversation if appropriate in order to help them understand why they did not gain the position. This conversation can be difficult for any manager, and involves a high level of understanding and tact, as well as the ability to provide guidance.

EXERCISE 10.1

As the chair of a selection committee, Keiko has to draw up clear criteria for evaluating the 100 written applications she has received for two entry-level library technician positions in her library. These are trainee positions, in which the successful applicants will spend 6 months in the three major areas of the library (public services, technical services, and special collections).

The number of applications has surprised and dismayed Keiko, who needs to bring the number down to 8 to 10 candidates to be invited for interviews. Write down some of the criteria Keiko might use to evaluate the written applications quickly and efficiently in order to get down to this number, bearing in mind the need to be fair and Keiko's accountability to the applicants.

Orienting New Staff

Once new staff members have been appointed, they arrive with a mixture of enthusiasm, attitudes, perceptions, and skills that must be managed to ensure that they meet the needs of the organization (with which they are unfamiliar) and their own needs and goals.

A detailed and comprehensive orientation program will help people new to the organization settle in quickly and comfortably, gaining a clear understanding of their rights and responsibilities, as well as those of the organization. During this period, important first impressions are formed and misconceptions over roles and duties may be easily dealt with.

 A good orientation yields long-term dividends in the form of committed staff and fewer problems for management.

An orientation program should be laid out in a written document, usually an interactive web based program, comprising a series of points that can be checked off and signed as completed, by both employee and manager. All new employees, regardless of level, should complete the checklist and sign it. The list should cover general procedures and policies common throughout the organization as well as specific activities related to the section employing the person.

Typical orientation checklists are shown on the following pages.

Personnel Files

The orientation checklists, together with the job application, interview notes, and references, form the first parts of the documentary record to be maintained for each employee. From then on, training activities, performance evaluations, counseling records, reprimands, probation reports, and sick and holiday leave information all have to be maintained in a personal and confidential file for that person. This file can be maintained by the manager (in smaller organizations) or by the human resources department in larger institutions. In either case, whether it is a physical file or online equivalent, completeness and confidentiality are vital.

THE REALLY IMPORTANT LIBRARY ORIENTATION CHECKLIST

Every new employee must complete and sign off this checklist within two weeks of starting with us. It should also be signed by the employee's direct supervisor and then submitted to the Human Resources area, within 14 days of the employee's starting date.

Attached to this general checklist should be a completed copy of the Section-specific list.

I have been briefed on:

The organization, its structure, and its mission ☐

Attendance hours, time sheets, sick and flex and holiday leave ☐

Occupational safety and health issues and responsibilities ☐

Harassment and mediation assistance ☐

Breaks and use of the staff room ☐

Proper maintenance of files and related records ☐

Mobile phone use ☐

Computer and Internet use ☐

Conflict of interest situations ☐

Ethical behavior ☐

Emergency evacuation procedures ☐

Fire wardens and first-aid officers ☐

I have been introduced to my colleagues, staff in related sections, ☐
and senior management

I have been given a tour of all areas of the organization ☐

I have been given an email account and organization sign-on ☐

Staff member...   Supervisor......................................

Date................

COLLECTION MAINTENANCE—STAFF ORIENTATION CHECKLIST

The Collection Maintenance Section is responsible for ensuring that all collection material is properly shelved or otherwise housed, and conducts regular programs to identify books and other items requiring conservation or preservation treatment.

I am aware of and understand the following work policies and practices that apply in the section, as well as the more general policies already explained in the main induction list:

Work practices

Safe lifting practices ☐

How to use the book trucks, handcarts, elevator, book lift, loading dock, and associated doors ☐

Emergency exits in the area ☐

How the schedule operates and whom to advise if I'm not going to be available for my normal shift ☐

Security procedures in the area ☐

Handling moldy or otherwise visibly deteriorated collection items ☐

Work policies

Heavy items (such as bound newspapers, large archive boxes) must be lifted and handled in accordance with the safe lifting practices. Always seek assistance when moving these items ☐

Safety boots are to be worn when working in the closed stacks, storage areas, or loading dock ☐

IDs are to be worn at all times. If an ID is lost it is your duty to advise security as soon as possible ☐

Record whereabouts on the main whiteboard at all times ☐

Advise supervisor when leaving work for the day ☐

Do not enter the closed-stack security area on your own ☐

I have read the above and acknowledge that I have received sufficient information and training to understand and implement these procedures and practices in my day-to-day work.

Staff member...   Supervisor.....................................

Date...............

Evaluation and Assessment

Orientation should also include advising new staff that there will be an evaluation of their performance within three to six months. This information is crucial in helping the organization and the individual better understand their needs and expectations. Allow plenty of time for this process, which should involve both a written report (detailed below) and discussion with the staff member involved.

From the organization's point of view, this is a good time to ensure that the new employee is performing to expectations. If this is the case, positive reinforcement and feedback will be appreciated by the person who may not have the experience to judge whether they have been doing a good job. It is also a chance for supervisors to express appreciation for the work done and to discuss development paths and opportunities for the individual. This should be a valuable, morale-building exercise.

If aspects of the person's work do not, in the eyes of the supervisor, meet the standard expected, this is the ideal time to address the problem. Discussing these issues with new employees is far easier than dealing with them when employees have been in the organization for a long time and may hold entrenched opinions, or feel from their experience that they know better. Addressing the problem of performance which does not meet expectations is dealt with later in this chapter. However, it is important to be clear before raising the issue that, as the manager or supervisor concerned, you fully understand the nature of the problem, are ready to listen to the staff member in a non-threatening and open manner, and have practical suggestions to assist in remedying the situation.

Performance Reports

An assessment or performance report usually covers both general competencies necessary for working successfully in the area and some specific skills related directly to the section or the job. The report will list a number of these general and specific criteria, with room for comment by the supervisor. Once completed, supervisor and employee go through the report, discussing the comments and addressing any of the issues raised.

A typical report will include headings such as:
- attendance (including punctuality, use of flextime, completion of time sheets, sick leave, and related issues)
- work as a team member (how well the person works with others, cooperation, helpfulness, willingness to learn, appropriate behavior toward supervisor and other team members)
- relations outside the team (working with senior management, courtesy to clients and others, telephone manner, responsiveness)
- quality of work (accuracy, level of output, presentation)
- attitude and approach (enthusiasm, interest, initiative, thoughtfulness, concentration, ability to work with limited direction)
- communication skills (both written and verbal).

It could also include job— or area—specific skills such as:
- use of specific software packages (quickness to learn)
- internal procedures, practices, and standards (quickness to learn, understanding, application).

There should then be an option for general comment on the employee's overall ability and recommendations for the next step, e.g., review in three months, transfer to normal review process, appoint permanently, etc.

Employees should add their own comments. Once completed, the evaluation and assessment tool should provide a valuable resource in developing staff and ensuring that both their own and the organization's needs are being met.

 EXERCISE 10.2

As the supervisor of a number of young people working as interns, you have to write individual assessments of their performance after the internships expire and to provide them with some self-knowledge that may help them gain permanent work.

You have decided to do this assessment under a series of headings that you can apply to each intern. List the major headings that you should use in order to provide the most useful feedback to these temporary staff members. Under each heading, give reasons for its inclusion and an example of what you might say.

Ongoing Performance Appraisal

While assessing performance is most important for new employees, some form of performance appraisal system is also desirable for continuing employees. Such systems aim to:

- identify and assess individual performance against previously agreed goals
- assist in promoting improved communications between managers and staff
- enable staff and managers to develop individual training and development programs
- assist managers to explain and promote corporate and business goals, and
- help individuals and the team increase effectiveness and productivity.

Some general principles relating to performance appraisal apply in all circumstances:

- having clear, measurable goals against which performance can be measured
- focusing on the factual
- being seen as a two-way process where the manager also listens
- being conducted in an atmosphere of mutual honesty, understanding, and trust
- being thoroughly prepared beforehand to ensure that the facts are clear
- being seen as a constructive exercise to benefit both employee and team objectives
- being timely and regular so as not to surprise the staff concerned.

Regular performance appraisal helps build a work environment that rewards goal achievement, emphasizes individual responsibility, and helps managers to identify and rectify problems before they become entrenched. However, it can also be challenging for staff who may see the process as intimidating, even threatening. Management must be sensitive to this and endeavor to ensure that staff view this as a constructive two-way process aimed at benefitting the employee and the organization.

If areas of concern are to be raised with a staff member, then this must be handled carefully in order to ensure the individual does not automatically switch into a defensive mode where they do not listen to the concern but focus on justifying themselves. This benefits no one. The aim is to ensure the staff member understands the issue and can see for his or herself that something needs to be done.

Staff Development

All staff—temporary, permanent, or volunteers—should expect their work to offer opportunities for personal development. With rapid change in most areas, training and retraining are an essential part of an organization's planning.

Training can take many forms, which include:

- organized courses on specific areas conducted in-house or externally
- on-the-job training provided by supervisors or co-workers
- regular time off to allow for further study
- attendance at workshops, conferences, and meetings of professional bodies
- job rotation or swapping staff with similar organizations
- enabling staff to take on new tasks or responsibilities, often as special projects.

In determining their needs, staff members should consider their short– and longer–term goals, and managers have to assess existing skills and performances against desired levels. Together, a training and development package relevant to the individual and the organization can be devised.

The benefits of a carefully constructed package include:
- increased skills and knowledge
- increased understanding and confidence
- improved motivation
- increased productivity and higher–quality work.

Training and development go hand in hand, and it is important for managers to accept, plan, and budget for the costs that accrue with a properly supported training and development program.

Counseling

Counseling is really the next, more formal step after feedback. It is not only related to discipline, but can also be a motivational tool to improve team morale and performance. Managers should not wait until a critical incident or situation arises before intervening, but should be on the alert for staff showing frustration, disillusionment, or other negative work attributes. Intervening at an early stage can help prevent small problems getting out of hand.

Managers have a responsibility to counsel staff members about work performance or behavior. If performance is affected by circumstances in their personal lives, it is not part of the manager's role to solve these problems. It some situations like these, staff should be advised to seek professional counseling help. Many organizations have a relationship with a counseling service, which provides some free sessions to employees in these situations. A manager should be aware of any such services in order to advise staff appropriately.

A manager should employ the following approach to most counseling situations:
- Decide beforehand whether counseling is to be informal (no written record) or formal (where notes will be taken and placed in a file). The first session is usually informal. Later sessions become formal if the situation has not changed but this will increase the stress associated with the process.
- Select a place that is private and free from distractions. It may be best to use a neutral place, rather than the manager's office.
- Allow ample time for the session.
- Usually, advise the person beforehand of what you wish to discuss so that they have time to prepare and can leave their workplace for that period. Occasionally, it may be necessary to act immediately (if their behavior is causing disruption) and prior notice will not be possible.
- A third party may also be present (often as a support for the staff member—this practice is quite acceptable and very useful in some emotional situations).
- Aim to arrive at an agreed-upon course of action—focus on the future, not the past.
- Concentrate on issues, not personalities; stay logical; be up-front and honest.
- Be patient and practice active listening and a caring attitude.

- Show respect for the other person and their concerns.
- Be clear on what is expected—the level of improvement in performance, the steps to be taken, and the timeframe in which they are to be achieved.
- If the session is to be written up, ensure that the staff member is aware of this. When the session has been written up, both parties should sign to accept the record or attach a dissenting version.
- Any written record must be placed in a confidential staff file and not disclosed without proper precautions.

If the problem behavior or performance does not change, an escalating set of steps may be appropriate depending upon the situation:

- consider changing the person's duties
- consider the possibilities of a transfer and a fresh start
- take more serious counseling steps involving personnel staff or senior management
- take formal disciplinary action.

Ensure that full written records are kept of all meetings and counseling sessions once these stages have been reached.

SCENARIO

In a small group, consider the following case study as if you were the manager or supervisor. Use the discussion in this chapter as a guide and brainstorm other ideas and options. You are expected to deliver a practical and workable solution that is in the best interests of the staff and the organization.

Elizabeth manages a small special library located in one large open-plan area. The staff has remained fairly constant for a number of years, and Graham and Michelle have worked together in the digitization team for three years. They have worked well and have proved an effective team.

Recently, however, Elizabeth has noticed an apparent strain in their relationship, and twice has heard them arguing quite loudly. Others in the office have also noticed and tend to avoid them. Elizabeth has noticed a change in their work output with targets regularly not being met. She is increasingly concerned due to the missed targets and because of the bad atmosphere that seems to surround them.

Elizabeth has tried talking in a casual way to Graham, the more senior of the two, but was basically told to mind her own business. She now feels the need for a sit-down session with one or both of them, to get to the bottom of the problem and improve the situation.

How should Elizabeth set up and run the session?

References and Further Reading

Dran, Gisella von, 'Human resources and leadership strategies for libraries in transition', *Library Administration and Management* 19:4, Fall 2005.

Fitsimmons, G., 'Library leadership column: Resource management: people: skills management', *The Bottom Line* 22:2, 2009.

Harper, Stephen, *Managing technostress in UK libraries: a realistic guide*, [online]. www.ariadne.ac.uk/issue25/technostress/

Heathfield, Susan M., *Performance management process checklist*, [online], 2012. http://humanresources.about.com/od/performancemanagement/a/perfmgmt.htm

Kieserman, R.H., 'Issues in library human resources management', *The Bottom Line* 21:4, 2008.

La Guardia, Cheryl, 'Professional development: what's it to you?' *Library Journal* March 20, 2014.

Larrivee, Anne, 'Exploring the stressors of new librarians', *Public Services Quarterly* 10:1, 2014.

McKay, Richard, 'Inspired hiring: tools for success', *Library Administration and Management* 20:3, Summer 2006.

Quast, Lisa, *Recruiting, reinvented: How companies are using social media in the hiring process*, [online], 2012. http://www.forbes.com/sites/lisaquast/2012/05/21/recruiting-reinvented-how-companies-are-using-social-media-in-the-hiring-process/

Wilkinson, Z.T., 'A human resources dilemma? Emergent themes in the experiences of part-time librarians', *Journal of Library Administration* 55:5, 2015.

CHAPTER ELEVEN
Building Effective Teams

Introduction

Managers achieve results through people. In virtually all organizations, this means building and leading effective teams. Few people work in isolation, and a good team supports and inspires its members, as well as being highly productive.

With the growing complexity of working environments, the rapid pace of change, and an increasing demand for higher efficiency and productivity, few individuals have the expertise or resources to complete a task alone. More than ever, the ability to work in a team is a critical success factor for employees looking to further their careers. For the organization, teams, not individuals, achieve objectives.

However, teams are made up of individuals with all their differences in background, personality, aptitude, education, and expectations. This is where a manager's skill is required to ensure that this diverse group forms an effective working unit. Diversity is important in building balanced teams with a range of strengths that lead to better decision-making, increased creativity, and improved problem-solving capabilities. This diversity is only one of a number of attributes that characterize effective teams.

Characteristics of an Effective Team

Parker (2008) notes that today, building and maintaining effective teams may be more difficult than ever due to the nature of the workplace. Teams may be virtual, with staff spread across many locations, or comprise a wide mix of culturally diverse members with different backgrounds and expectations—all working together in a high-pressure, results-oriented environment. He summarizes effective teams as comprising 'effective team players' (p. 59) and goes on to note twelve characteristics that distinguish successful teams and their players:

- clear purpose
- informality
- participation
- listening skills
- civilized disagreement
- consensus decisions
- open communication
- clear roles and work assignments
- shared leadership
- external relations
- style diversity
- self-assessment (p. 62).

Clear Purpose

Clearly defined aims and objectives are the guiding principles upon which the team focuses its activities. These include short-term and long-term goals that have been set in consultation with the team (not imposed upon it) and provide the framework within which the team conducts its activities.

Informality

In such a climate team members are confident and encouraged to speak out, ask questions, seek clarification and use initiative to bring in new ideas. They are willing to take risks and, due to the ease of communication among them, are ready to help others where necessary. An informal climate leads to a comfortable atmosphere where staff enjoy their work and participate fully in reaching objectives.

Participation

Participation is encouraged by an informal atmosphere. The effective team draws on a wide range of expertise, leading to greater satisfaction among those involved, and a better result for the organization. Managers have to learn to manage the level of participation by providing opportunities for quieter team members to become involved, and by channeling the energies of the more forceful.

Listening Skills

According to Parker (p. 80) "the single most important factor distinguishing effective from ineffective teams is the ability of team members to listen to each other". Team members have a responsibility to respect each other's views and listen to each other's arguments. Managers have to model this behavior by practicing effective listening skills and promoting their use among other team members.

Civil Disagreement

Disagreements or conflicts naturally arise in an open team encouraged to speak out in an informal atmosphere. If not dealt with effectively, they can be destabilizing. When disagreements do occur, they should be expressed in a manner that relates directly to the issue at hand, not in a generalized or personal way. Dealing with the issue requires team members to acknowledge that disagreements are acceptable—and often the only way to reach the best solution. By offering alternatives, encouraging flexibility among staff, defusing difficult situations with humor, and emphasizing how everyone is trying to attain the same solution, managers can play a leading role in ensuring that disagreement is a positive process.

Consensus Decisions

Consensus is a form of group decision based on unity, not necessarily unanimity. Particularly on key decisions, it is important that team members feel they have had the opportunity to express their opinions. They need to feel these have been listened to and their objections considered and answered. While they may not all agree with the final decision, they understand why it was made and accept it. If the team functions well, consensus decisions will be supported and respected.

Open Communication

Team members must trust each other and their manager sufficiently to speak out openly on issues, without fear of embarrassment or hostile reactions. An informal atmosphere encourages open communication, and managers must foster it by inviting discussion of issues and reacting in a nonjudgmental manner to the range of opinions offered.

Clear Roles and Work Assignments

Team members have roles that need to be understood clearly by their colleagues and manager. Understanding one's role affects expectations of what one can or cannot do, as well as one's sense of self. Roles are different from work assignments relating to tasks (which are usually clearly understood), and if the team is to function effectively, there must be clarification and acceptance of roles and what they entail.

Shared Leadership

While all teams have a formal head or leader, all members should feel responsible for both successes and failures. In a trusting environment, all members have input into team activities and share its achievements. Team managers must ensure that they build a culture that advocates this approach and supports the sharing of responsibility, while handling administrative and bureaucratic tasks related to their position.

External Relations

Effective teams build close relationships with others within and outside the organization in order to further their aims. This networking indicates a strong, confident team that values outside input and customer feedback. It is also useful in building a wider understanding of the work of the team and maintaining its profile in the broader organizational or professional community.

Style Diversity

Teams are made up of individuals with different attitudes and aptitudes. Good teams enjoy a mix of talents, in substance and in style, leading to better results. A team of practical 'hands-on' workers may have difficulty looking at the big picture and spending time on planning, while a team of planners and organizers may take too long to make decisions and get to work. Managers must ensure that, as far as possible, there is a mix of talents in their team and that differences are respected.

Self-Assessment

Teams should be able to assess their progress and effectiveness regularly. Managers should ensure periods of 'time out' to enable the team to step aside from the day-to-day and consider their achievements. Fundamentally, an effective team needs to ask occasionally, "What can we do to improve?"

EXERCISE 11.1

Marion is the head of a team of six library support staff planning a regional conference for library support staff. She is concerned about the size of the job, their inexperience in organizing a major conference, and the tight time schedule. In order for everything to come together on time and according to expectations, Marion will have to have a highly effective team. Using the headings below, note at least two strategies under each that Marion could adopt to help build her winning team.

Clear purpose

Clear roles and work assignments

External relations

Consensus decisions

Shared leadership

Effective listening skills

Role of a Good Team Leader

A completely effective team must also have a leader who accepts the role with enthusiasm and shares the task with the team. However, the leader must be ready to take full responsibility for the success or failure of the team and to consider the impact of all actions on the team. Parker (p. 114) suggests that the responsibilities of a good team leader comprise:

- seeking and gathering of information
- initiating
- clarifying
- harmonizing
- encouraging
- coordinating.

Information

Team leaders must seek out the necessary information for successful completion of the task. They can use this as the basis to offer opinions, propose actions and explain why something needs to be done. Providing such data to the team provides them with the information they need to participate effectively in the decision-making process. It can also act as a catalyst, encouraging other team members to provide additional information or data relevant to the task at hand.

Initiating

Proposing goals and objectives and initiating tasks is a major role for team leaders. They are responsible for getting things done and must take a leading role in working with the team to determine the best way forward in dealing with a task or an issue. They need to guide this process to ensure problems are foreseen (as far as possible) and resources in place to enable successful completion of any project without undue stress being placed on team members.

Clarifying

Clarifying and reinforcing the importance of goals, procedures, or tasks is a necessary role for the team leader. In any complex project, questions arise, objectives may be forgotten or lost, misunderstandings occur, and conflicting advice could be offered. The leader needs to work through these difficulties, interpreting and understanding the issues raised, and seeking team consensus in progressing towards their goals. As part of this process, regular 'reality testing' of ideas or proposals is a useful approach to ensuring their practicality.

Harmonizing

In order to reduce tension and overcome difficulties and conflicts, the team leader must arbitrate, compromise, and reconcile different views and opinions. In order to maintain productivity, harmony within the team is a critical asset.

Encouraging

Being responsive, enthusiastic, and supportive of the team members and their work is a vital role for the leader. From the leader's example, the team members take on a positive approach to the work and each other, maximizing their potential to achieve.

Coordinating

Where a number of different tasks are required to achieve the overall objective, the team leader needs to ensure that all the work is completed at appropriate times, that resources are available when required, and that the goal of one group does not conflict with the goal of another. Standards and consistency in the quality of work must also be maintained—sometimes challenging when team members may be geographically dispersed.

Exercising these skills will help the team reach its objectives and help the team leader build a positive, achievement-oriented work group that is confident, self-directed, successful, and viewed by its members as providing a good working environment.

Coping with Problems in the Team

Since teams are groups of individuals, it is inevitable that occasionally, even in the best managed teams, problems will arise that have an adverse effect on the team's functioning. It is important that these be dealt with quickly and effectively. Some problems will be strictly individual, others team-wide. The following strategies may be effective in either situation:

- coaching
- counseling
- team building
- change of assignments.

Coaching

The team leader may need to 'coach' individual team members who are having difficulties in reaching their goals, performing the task within agreed deadlines, or understanding the requirements of the work. This is a non-threatening, supportive role that the team leader can adopt to build commitment and enthusiasm, as well as to improve the technical or work practices of the individual concerned.

Counseling

Counseling is used with individual team members who are not contributing and have a negative view of the team's activities. It is important that the team member in question has the opportunity to express concerns to the team leader and that these concerns are addressed seriously. If problems continue, it must be made clear to the individual that the negative impact of his or her behavior has to be resolved. It may be that the only solution is removal from the team.

Team Building

Team building is a technique used to help in overcoming longer-term problems in teams. It can also be used with fully functioning teams to improve effectiveness. Usually team building involves the group's going off-site for a period to work through and analyze why it is not achieving its full potential. This process will be facilitated by an external consultant (who, importantly, should be seen as a neutral party) experienced in working through these issues.

Team building is appropriate when
- there is a loss of production or general reduction in the quality of service
- customer complaints increase
- conflict and hostility between team members are evident
- team meetings are poorly attended and ineffective in making decisions
- there is apathy and loss of enthusiasm
- complaints are common, and the leader receives increasingly negative feedback
- tasks or activities are not completed on time or are continually put off.

Change of Assignments

If the team is not succeeding as well as expected on a particular task, consider taking a break and developing an exciting short-term objective that most team members will adopt enthusiastically. A change of pace and scene may make a considerable difference in the level of interest and morale. Before returning to the original task, have a brainstorming session to devise new work practices or procedures to make this task more interesting and challenging.

EXERCISE 11.2

Huong is the supervisor of a cataloging team comprising eight staff. They have been together for a number of years with few changes. The last year or so has seen productivity falling and, while there is no obvious disharmony, Huong feels that somehow the team is in a negative mood and has certainly lost enthusiasm. She feels that a team-building exercise may be necessary, but first she wishes to try to handle the problem herself. Note under the following headings the steps she might take to try to improve the situation:

Information

Initiating

Clarifying

Harmonizing

Encouraging

Coordinating and controlling

SCENARIO

In a small group, consider the following case study as if you were the manager or supervisor. Use the discussion in this chapter as a guide and brainstorm other ideas and options. You are expected to deliver a practical and workable solution that is in the best interests of the staff and the organization.

Stephanie and Frank head the cataloging and reader services sections of a community college library. They both have small teams working for them in a positive and effective manner. During the approaching holidays, the entire collection will have to be moved, as the library is relocating to larger premises.

No money is available for additional help, so the move will have to be done principally by members of the two teams. No one in either team is enthusiastic about the job, and Stephanie and Frank have received complaints from disgruntled staff who want to be left to get on with their own jobs.

How could the two supervisors go about building commitment to the task and generating enthusiasm among the two teams? How will they go about getting both teams to work together and to pool their skills effectively in order to achieve a timely and successful move?

References and Further Reading

Caron, Alan R., *Managing teams effectively*, [online], 2004.
http://www.alancaron.com/articles/MANAGING%20TEAMS%20EFFECTIVELY.pdf

D. Hall-Ellis Sylvia, 'Reward systems promote high-performance work teams achieving library mission', *The Bottom Line* 27:2, 2014.

Kanaga, Kim & Michael E. Kossler, *How to form a team: five keys to high performance*, Greensboro, NC., Center for Creative Leadership, 2001.

Keiser, B.E, 'Tools will keep us together: collaboration for library teams', *Online Searcher* 38:1, 2014.

Knecht, Mike, 'Virtual teams in libraries', *Library Administration and Management* 18:1, Winter 2004.

McNamara, Carter, *All about team building*, [online].
http://managementhelp.org/groups/team-building.htm

Parker, Glenn M., *Team players and teamwork: new strategies for developing successful collaborations*, 2nd ed., San Francisco, Jossey-Bass, 2008.

Porter, Brandi, 'Managing with emotional intelligence', *Library Leadership and Management* 24:4, 2010.

CHAPTER TWELVE
Financial Management

Introduction

Managing money and budgets is generally simpler than managing staff. Yet managers often spend more time and effort worrying about finances than about staffing. This is probably due to the high visibility of financial matters, and the guidelines and controls imposed on spending—far more obvious than the more flexible approach needed to manage staff. In addition, budgetary controls are a simple yet useful way for management to monitor and evaluate projects and to judge performance. Most libraries and information centers need systems of financial management that are straightforward to implement and maintain.

Money management and budgeting, in every form, should relate to the core of the library or information center functions. Spending must be directed toward organizational aims and objectives. There is a very close relationship between budgeting, strategic planning, and spending. The budget forms an essential part of planning and control, whereby:

- the cost of providing any service can be estimated reliably
- spending is assessed against particular activities or programs
- comparisons are made among the cost-effectiveness of such programs
- planning future activities is made possible in the light of expected income and expenditure.

For most libraries and information centers, budgets are subsets of a far larger corporate budget covering the whole organization. They compete with other sections for a share of the corporate 'pie'. Regularly, the library or information center has to make a strong case to maintain or improve its funding, in the face of competing demands from seemingly more critical sectors.

It is a very demanding task of the manager to ensure that library and information center programs are properly promoted, tied to broader corporate goals, directly relevant and visible to senior management, cost-effective, and carefully budgeted and controlled. Not only is this necessary for survival; for many organizations it is a legal requirement.

Public Funding

Most libraries and information centers rely heavily on government funding (federal, state, or local), to continue their operations. The ups and downs of public funding impact on how programs are costed out, funding is sought, and records are maintained.

When government agencies implement fee-for-service principles, some libraries and information centers find themselves more and more concerned with maintaining adequate funding to enable them to provide their services. In addition, with the explosive growth of new services driven primarily by developments in technology, funding new initiatives is a major concern.

Thus it becomes more important than ever to ensure value for money by proper budgeting for activities, careful cost-benefit research, and (for new services) budget-neutral charging.

Accountability and auditability are also primary requirements for any publicly funded institution. Taxpayers have a right to know where their money is spent. For managers, it is essential to ensure that complete and accurate records of income and expenditure are maintained to enable proper reporting. Good record keeping is straightforward and simple—and a serious responsibility.

Another aspect of managing the budget relates to the annual cycle of appropriation. Funding for most activities is provided on an annual basis and is accountable over the same period. It is the manager's job to take this annual cycle into account when planning projects that may last longer than one year or which may not come into operation before the end of the fiscal year. Cash flow should be controlled throughout the budget cycle in order to ensure that funds are properly spent before the end of the period, while ensuring funds at appropriate times for all the projects planned for the year.

Discretionary and Nondiscretionary Monies

Budget allocations may at first glance appear to be large amounts that offer the organization a wide array of options. However, most of the money allocated is usually for operations over which lower-level management has little control.

Nondiscretionary Funding

Money known as nondiscretionary funding is earmarked for areas such as:
- building lease or rental payments
- power costs (electricity, air conditioning, etc.)
- staff salaries, leave, retirement benefits
- insurance of various types
- other expenses that are difficult or impossible to alter in the short term.

A local manager has little or no control over this expenditure—i.e., no discretion as to how it is spent in the short to medium term.

Discretionary Funding

After taking nondiscretionary expenses into account, typically 10 percent or less of the budget allocated to an area is available for projects that are controllable by management in the short term. This limitation has to be considered carefully whenever expensive, long-term projects are planned, in order to ensure sufficient cash flow to enable the project to be completed.

Fixed and Variable Costs

An important and related concept is the difference between fixed and variable costs. When calculating the true cost of any program, it is necessary to appreciate the proportions of fixed and variable costs involved, in order to plan any expansion or contraction of activity.

Fixed Costs

Fixed costs are incurred by the organization in pursuing its goals and are not affected by minor, short-term fluctuations in workload. These costs relate to such matters as:

- lease or rental of premises
- insurance and maintenance agreements
- heating and lighting
- staff salaries.

These costs change only very occasionally, and will not be affected if, say, a few more books are cataloged one year or additional material is digitized.

Variable Costs

Variable costs, however, change directly in relation to the work done and are not set in any way—they can range from zero to any amount and are more directly controllable by management in the short term. Thus, for instance:

- The number of books bought or serials subscribed to in any year is a variable that can easily be changed, should management decide to cut back.
- The number of items being given conservation treatment can be reduced.
- The amount of overtime made available to staff can also be varied depending upon the budget situation.

 EXERCISE 12.1

The Uptown Public Library is considering introducing a bookmobile service in order to serve its remote users better. The library intends to purchase and convert a large van. The bookmobile will be stocked with materials from existing collections.

What are the fixed costs involved in setting up the service?

What are the variable costs?

What are the long-term implications for the library?

Forms of Budgeting

Budgeting requires planning, organizing, and controlling skills to ensure that:

- plans and proposed activities are properly costed out
- appropriate financial resources are allocated to an activity
- performance can be measured against the cost involved.

When preparing budgets and making a case for funding, a number of budgeting methods can be adopted. Usually these are dictated by the needs of the parent organization, which requires budgets to be presented and argued for in a particular manner. Methods of presenting budgets include:

- incremental budgeting
- program-based budgeting
- zero-based budgeting.

Incremental Budgeting

Incremental budgeting looks at the previous year's allocation for a particular task and makes a bid for the new funds based on that experience and the expectations of what will happen in the coming year. Thus, if $4,000 was allocated to cover OCLC costs in Year 1, and the library actually spent this amount, the cataloging manager may adopt an incremental approach and ask for $4,400, in the expectation that OCLC charges may rise, or the library's use of OCLC may increase.

Program-Based Budgeting

Program-based budgeting (PBB) considers all the activities or programs in an area and works out how much it costs to run these programs. Budget requests are then based upon the size and nature of the program planned for the coming year. The advantages of this approach are that a more accurate picture of the actual cost of running a particular activity is gained, and more consideration may be given to how projects compare with one another.

Zero-Based Budgeting

Zero-based budgeting (ZBB) is similar to program-based budgeting in that it endeavors to apportion costs to a program or activity. However, ZBB requires managers to evaluate their programs each year and to budget as if they were starting from scratch, or base zero, for the coming year's costs. Thus it effectively requires a complete evaluation of all activities every year.

The Business Case

As part of the budgeting process, new initiatives or even the continuation of existing ones may need more support than a simple financial breakdown. Thus a business case may need to be developed that gathers together an evidence base to support what is proposed and importantly, think about alternatives and what is now not going to be done as a result of taking this new action. Essentially you should be trying to prove that this new project or continuing activity is the best use of the scarce funds available to you in order to meet your organizational goals.

A business case will consider options and alternatives and provide a cost/benefit analysis of the preferred approach which will emphasize the rationale for adopting this plan of action. Note that cost/benefit analysis will usually have to consider long term or ongoing costs as well as the more obvious start-up costs in order to come up with realistic budget estimates over time. Quantifying in dollar terms benefits such as improved customer service can be difficult, but nonetheless does need to be considered and some form of metric determined in order to provide an effective analysis.

EXERCISE 12.2

Meg is planning to introduce a new product in her school media center/library. It is to be a school kit aimed at teenagers, covering all aspects of global warming and climate change. Her school system uses a program-based budgeting method, and in order to present her proposal, Meg has to have it fully costed out. Think about the costs that are likely to be involved in putting the product together, and apportion them under the following groupings:

Research

Production

Marketing and promotion

Maintaining Financial Records

Keeping track of expenditures is an important part of the manager's work. If done accurately and methodically, it is simple.

Essentially, proper financial management requires the maintenance of records regarding income, expenditure, and encumbrances. Encumbrances are orders placed with suppliers that have not yet been filled or paid for, but which are expected to be charged within the accounting period. Keeping track of encumbrances and following up with suppliers are necessary to ensure that goods or services are received and paid for in the financial period in which they are encumbered.

The use of spreadsheet software makes the organizing and control of financial information very straightforward and gives managers a clear idea, throughout the year, of their financial position.

Purchasing

Purchasing requires managers to exercise particular care to ensure that the acquisition of materials or services is done correctly. Most organizations have strict guidelines as to how to buy goods and services and what may be purchased by staff at varying levels.

Delegation of Authority

'Delegation of authority' is the term used when disbursing authority is given (delegated) to a manager at a particular level. For instance, as a section supervisor you may be delegated disbursing authority for $500, allowing you to purchase items up to that amount without permission from your supervisor. The head of the library may have a delegation of authority for $10,000 without permission from a superior.

Procedures

As well as rules about delegations of authority, there are usually strict guidelines about procedures. The procedure for purchasing an item is usually spelled out clearly. It may be that if the item costs less than $100 it may be purchased from whoever is thought to be the best source. If the item costs (say) between $100 and $1,000, not only is it necessary to have the correct delegation of authority to authorize its purchase, but you may also be required to prove that you have 'shopped around' for it, and that this price is competitive. Between $1,000 and $5,000 you may be required to obtain written quotes and to write up in detail why one has been selected over others. Over (say) $5,000, it may be necessary to advertise and go through a formal bidding process.

None of the usual purchasing procedures for lower-priced materials and services is complex or time consuming. However, managers must ensure that all relevant paperwork is completed and records properly maintained. Otherwise managers leave themselves open to questions and allegations that will be difficult to answer. Controlling financial activity is relatively easy in most organizations, and, with regular audits, managers are very exposed if they do not follow the rules.

SCENARIO

In a small group, consider the following case study as if you were the manager or supervisor. Use the discussion in this chapter as a guide and brainstorm other ideas and options. You are expected to deliver a practical and workable solution that is in the best interests of the staff and the organization.

Michaela is considering the purchase of a 3D printer to be set up in the school library and managed by library staff. This will be a significant investment of $20k in order to obtain a robust printer and consumables sufficient to meet the needs of a wide range of users – from the Art and Science departments to IT students.

Michaela is putting together a business case to be presented to the School Board. She has to consider the costs (both one-off and ongoing) and benefits arising from purchasing the equipment, making a case for its acquisition.

Develop a business case for the purchase of the printer considering the following aspects:

Who will benefit and how – can this be measured in money terms?

How this fits in with the overall objectives of the Library

The fixed and variable costs (immediate and longer-term)

Whether any savings may be made elsewhere to help fund the project

References and Further Reading

Elliott, D.S. *Measuring your library's value: how to do a cost-benefit analysis for your public library*, Chicago, ALA, 2007.

Hallam, Arlita W. & Teresa R. Dalston, *Managing budgets and finances: a how-to-do-it manual for librarians*, New York, Neal-Schuman, 2005.

Holley, Robert P., 'Library planning and budgeting: A few underappreciated principles', *Journal of Library Administration* 54:8, 2014.

Martin Prosperity Institute, *So much more: the economic impact of the Toronto Public Library on the City of Toronto*, [online], 2013.
http://www.torontopubliclibrary.ca/content/about-the-library/pdfs/board/meetings/2013/dec09/10_1.pdf

Matthews, Joseph R., 'Valuing information, information services, and the library: possibilities and realities', *Libraries and the Academy,* 13:1, 2013.

McKay, Duncan, *Effective financial planning for library and information services*, 2nd ed., London, Europa Publications, 2003.

Public Records Office of Victoria, *Writing a business case*, [online], 2010.
http://prov.vic.gov.au/wp-content/uploads/2011/05/1010g4.pdf

CHAPTER THIRTEEN
Creating Quality Service

Introduction

Any library, information center, or related organization is in the business of providing a service to its clients. The success or failure of that service will be judged more on the quality than the quantity of interactions. It is characteristic of all service organizations that quality depends upon the individual who delivers it, and the expectations of those receiving it, making it hard to ensure consistency and high standards in every transaction.

Unlike a manufacturing concern where the same item can be mass produced to exactly the same standards thousands of times, services cannot be mass produced, since they cannot be stored. Each transaction is a one-time event, usually 'consumed' in front of the deliverer. If the crucial client/staff interaction that comprises the delivery of service is faulty in some way, it is apparent to both parties immediately and may lead to dissatisfied clients, provoking loss of business, unhappy staff, and long-term problems.

Remember that there are major costs involved in not providing quality service. In order to avoid them, a manager must be concerned with:
- understanding client needs
- providing the right service to meet these needs
- implementing a good delivery system to ensure that service is appropriate and timely
- balancing the books
- ensuring a constant commitment to organizational goals.

Unfortunately, most managers become removed from dealing with clients face to face. In many organizations, dealing with clients is treated as lower-level work, and junior staff are assigned to it. The result is that managers forget how stressful and demanding it is to handle questions that range from the trivial to the complex, to deal often with strangers, and to meet the sometimes hostile or sarcastic response of a dissatisfied client. Yet this interaction is possibly the most crucial work done in the organization. Without a client base, there would be no need for the organization.

 Managers must remember that a loyal client base is as much an asset as any physical item. Maintaining and expanding that base is fundamental to their whole purpose.

Understanding the Customer

Maintaining and expanding one's client/customer base involves understanding not only what your customer is asking for at a particular moment, but also meeting or exceeding his or her general expectations for the service. It is also crucial to be clear as to who constitutes your customer base. You must therefore define who is your customer, and who is not, and what you can offer that the competition cannot.

The 'customer experience' concept has evolved in recent years, primarily focused on the commercial world but equally relevant to the non-profit sector such as libraries. A way of viewing this has been proposed by Besednjak (2011) who takes Maslow's famous hierarchy of needs concept to envisage a 'customer satisfaction pyramid'. Starting from the bottom, his version of Maslow's hierarchy focuses on why customers will do business with you, and come back again and again — if their needs are met in the right way.

Level 1. Service is provided in a timely and satisfactory manner meeting the basic expectations of the customer.

Level 2. Additional aspects of the customer experience occur with friendly, knowledgeable, consistent and caring staff providing added value.

Level 3. Connecting with the customer at an emotional level—be professional in your approach and caring, concerned and helpful. Have you really met their needs?

Level 4. Make the customer experience fun and enjoyable—something they want to repeat. The aim is for them to become advocates for your service, taking opportunities to praise and recommend the work you do, and in the process becoming an important political ally.

Remember that while for you it may be just another customer, for the customer this may be a one-off experience, or a vitally important part of their day. Making that experience memorable can have a real impact on them. Thus moving customers up this pyramid is a central aim of quality service.

To understand your customer's needs fully, listen carefully and don't be afraid to ask questions. Clients may be unsure what they need, staff may misinterpret what is said, and both will make mistakes. It is therefore crucial in ensuring a satisfactory outcome that the right question is being answered.

In order to gain insight into customer needs, undertake formal or informal surveys. This can range from simply sitting down with a regular client to discuss the client's requirements and how well they are being met, to sending survey questionnaires to users and potential users asking how they feel about the range and quality of services provided. For nonusers, surveys or personal contact can be useful in finding out why they do not use the service and may suggest ways of tailoring the service more directly to their requirements.

Another outcome of more fully understanding customer needs will be the ability to group them into general categories. This will help in providing services designed for their specific requirements and act as a guide to the necessary level of timeliness and depth required by that group.

Providing the Right Service

With a clearer understanding of client needs it should be possible to design a product or service appropriate to their requirements. In doing this, staff must be committed also to an ethic that views quality service as the preeminent part of their job. For managers, this means employing customer-oriented staff who are willing and able to commit to the ideals inherent in putting the customer first.

To emphasize the importance of excellence in service, a customer service policy should be drawn up, publicized, and promoted to all staff. Existing employees should have input into the development of such a policy. New employees must be given copies of the policy and be expected to read it and support its aims.

The policy should cover areas such as:
- the various client groups and their requirements
- timeliness and quality indicators
- level of response expected
- training rights and responsibilities
- handling difficult situations, etc.

Being responsive to changing client needs may require the following internal changes:
- redesigning systems and practices
- redeploying staff from one area to another
- providing training in technical aspects of the work
- providing personal development courses to improve the level of interpersonal skills
- redesigning office space
- ensuring appropriate backup procedures
- ensuring adequate staff are on duty when demand is heaviest
- providing new services or withdrawing old ones
- developing feedback mechanisms to enable evolving customer requirements to be monitored and demands anticipated.

 EXERCISE 13.1

Allan has just taken over as the manager of a large university's archives. The aim of the archives is to seek out and preserve a wide variety of material relating to the university's 100-year history. He assumes that his client base is mainly faculty and administration, but also believes there might be other potential clients within the broader community.

As one of his first tasks, Allan has been asked to draw up a user service policy that will provide the university administration with a clearer picture of what services the archives provides. Allan believes that unless he produces a very positive document, his funding is likely to be cut in next year's budget.

Using the headings below as current or potential customer groups that could make use of the archives' collections, explain how they might use its resources and what priority they could expect for their inquiries.

University administration

University academics

Graduate students

Undergraduate students

Local press or other media

National press or other media

The public

The Service Delivery System

Once the nature and level of service have been determined, it is necessary to consider the manner in which it is to be delivered. This delivery mechanism will depend very much upon the service provided and the nature of the organization. Once again, the basics of a quality delivery system will tie in closely with organizational culture and the stated aims and objectives of the customer service policy.

General issues to consider when developing the mechanism include:

- understanding where customers are located and any special, localized requirements
- the level of technology available to assist with service delivery and the client's technical sophistication—e.g., there is no point in delivering a response to someone in the form of large computer files if the client lacks the high-speed connectivity to open them easily
- having systems flexible enough to respond to urgent or unusual requests while at the same time providing consistency in service
- training staff in the interpersonal communication skills required for face-to-face or remote delivery
- having policies and procedures in place and staff properly trained to deal with dissatisfied customers
- ensuring that clients understand what is being delivered—e.g., does the library clear copyright on a photograph that someone wishes to include in a book, or is it the client's responsibility?
- a clear understanding of who pays any delivery costs.

 Well thought-out and smooth delivery will add significantly to customer satisfaction and is a basic ingredient for building a quality service.

Balancing the Books

Any level of customer service comes at a cost. At the same time, not providing a quality service also incurs costs. These costs must be balanced against each other when developing service standards and delivery mechanisms. Inevitably this balancing leads to the development of priorities and the provision of varying levels of service, depending on the perceived importance of the service in relation to organizational goals.

Issues to be considered when deciding upon the quality and depth of service offered include:

- the customer group and its power to affect the operation of the organization—e.g., a local library board member may well get a quicker turnaround on her inquiries at the public library than a student using the same facility
- the aims and objectives of the organization and how the service supports them—i.e., the closer the link with 'core mission', the more central the service is to the organization
- the actual cost (time and other resources) involved in delivering the service
- the potential for the service to win significant support, provide publicity, engender new business, or otherwise promote the organization

- the added value that the service may bring to the organization by developing staff skills, adding to an existing knowledge base, making new contacts, or widening professional networks and creating enthusiasm and motivation among staff.

All these issues, as well as the more obvious costs and benefits, must be taken into account when 'balancing the books' on quality service.

Building Commitment

If the customer service policy is properly developed—client groups identified, services designed well, priorities described clearly, and delivery mechanisms explained properly—the blueprint will support the achievement of organizational aims. With committed staff, clear goals, and regular reviews, quality service can be provided that will undoubtedly assist in raising overall organizational performance.

 EXERCISE 13.2

Ali works in a busy museum research center. The museum is nationally recognized and deals with inquiries from members of the public, politicians, and media groups such as TV broadcasters, journalists, etc. In order to improve the quality of service offered to these client groups, Ali is developing guidelines that will form the basis of a formal customer service policy. The guidelines cover the areas listed below. Note after each heading the sort of things Ali will be concerned with in developing the guidelines.

Customer groupings

Priorities

Levels of service

Costs/benefits

Staffing implications

SCENARIO

In a small group, consider the following case study as if you were the manager or supervisor. Use the discussion in this chapter as a guide and brainstorm other ideas and options. You are expected to deliver a practical and workable solution that is in the best interests of the staff and the organization.

Ricardo works on the reference desk at the New Town Public Library. He has held the position for some years and has noticed that the nature of questions has gradually changed.

Previously, most clients asked for particular books, subjects, or authors (questions easily answered from the catalog), were concerned about mundane issues such as the location of the nearest restroom or phone, or were looking for maps of the local area. However, more recently, Ricardo has been asked for information regarding social security benefits, unemployment and job security issues (including two questions about unfair dismissal), and for local organizations' annual reports. He has felt somewhat inadequate in answering some of these questions.

Ricardo comes to see you, the head of reference services, and is concerned about not being able to provide the level or quality of service that he feels these clients deserve. He seems distressed by this, and you are concerned about how he will cope if the situation continues.

What steps could you undertake to try to help?

📖 References and Further Reading

Besednjak, Frank, *The customer satisfaction pyramid*, [online], 2011.
http://contractingbusiness.com/archive/customer-satisfaction-pyramid

Hernon, Peter & John R. Whitman, *Delivering satisfaction and service quality: A customer based approach for libraries*, Chicago, American Library Association, 2001.

Library Research Service, *Library user survey templates & how-tos*, [online], 2013.
http://www.lrs.org/library-user-surveys-on-the-web/

Michelli, Joseph A., *The new gold standard: 5 leadership principles for creating a legendary customer experience courtesy of the Ritz-Carlton Hotel Company*, New York, McGraw Hill, 2008.

Museums Libraries and Archives Council (MLA), *What do the public want from libraries*, [online], 2010.
http://www.artscouncil.org.uk/media/uploads/mla_research_files/what_public_want_from_libraries_full_research_report_final_081110.pdf

OCLC Web Junction, *Extreme customer service, every time*, [online], 2013.
http://www.webjunction.org/events/webjunction/Extreme_Customer_Service_Every_Time.html

Pew Research Center, *Library services in the digital age*, [online], 2013.
http://libraries.pewinternet.org/2013/01/22/library-services/

Verzosa, Fe Angela, *Delivering service quality and satisfying library customers in a changing environment*, [slides], [online], 2011.
http://www.slideshare.net/verzosaf/delivering-service-quality-and-satisfying-library-customers-in-a-changing-environment

CHAPTER FOURTEEN
Marketing

Introduction

Marketing is not selling. Selling is convincing the public to buy your product or service without concern as to whether it is what they actually need. Marketing approaches the situation in the opposite way by identifying the goods or services required by consumers and marketing accordingly. Customer requirements are paramount, not the product or service the organization produces.

Anyone who has dealt with computer companies will have heard the jargon 'solutions'. These companies are not selling hardware or software, but offering solutions to an existing problem—a clear example of the marketing approach. Libraries and information centers, too, must be in the business of providing solutions to users' needs.

The aim of marketing is to turn consumers who have a present or potential need for your service into customers who use it. A good example is a special library in a government department—there is a large consumer base (the employees of the organization) but typically only a few are customers. It is a marketing challenge for library management to increase that number.

Moving Consumers to Customers

To help change consumers into customers, the following steps should be undertaken:
- analyze the environment
- develop a service
- test the service
- package, distribute, and promote
- monitor progress.

Analyze the Environment

Analyzing the environment is commonly done for many aspects of planning—remember the SWOT analysis in Chapter 2 of this book. To assist in developing marketing plans, the analysis will concentrate on identifying potential customers or markets.

eg For example,

- do they exist in a limited area (government department, school, university, local service area) or are they spread more widely?
- are there restrictions to moving out from your identified consumer base or can a service be targeted to a new market?—e.g., academic libraries frequently allow non-students to enroll as restricted users if they pay a fee
- are some groups more likely customers than others?

Develop a Service

Develop a product or service that is congruent with consumer demands and organizational goals. Maintaining and regularly reviewing this link is crucial. As organizational goals change, the library must revisit its marketing strategies.

eg   For example, new legislation is introduced that will impact on the work of a government agency. The agency's library identifies a consumer demand for a simple summary of the changes and their impact. The library then devises a summary or outline that is used to update the agency's relevant web pages, or even as the basis of a print information brochure. This new service is provided while something else, once considered important, gets lower priority.

Test the Service

Always market-test a new product or service with a small group before embarking on full-scale promotion. Ensure that management support and approval are obtained and that 'market champions'—key users who have influence in the organization—are vocal supporters.

Package, Distribute, and Promote

Style and presentation are vital in launching and promoting new or improved services—invest some time, effort, and money in this activity. The aim is to tempt consumers into trying the product—not just to tell them about it. Make sure all library staff are aware of the promotion and can answer questions or provide any help that may be required by potential users.

Monitor Progress

Like all plans, any marketing strategy must be monitored and its success measured. All products and services have a life cycle that has to be assessed. What is popular, relevant, and meeting users' needs one year may not be in two years' time. Thus, monitoring the progress of any initiative is important to keeping it relevant and providing early warning if demand is falling away.

These steps can help in building and maintaining a customer base, although long-term viability is best ensured by a longer-term marketing plan that becomes a major plank in the strategic plan for the organization.

Strategic Marketing

When developing long-term strategic marketing plans, more effort needs to be taken in identifying opportunities, considering costs and the competition, and evaluating the impact of the strategy on existing programs. The following major variables need detailed investigation:

- market opportunities
- market segments
- competition
- marketing mix.

Market Opportunities

Identifying opportunities—i.e., consumer needs—can be done by questionnaires, face-to-face discussion, telephone interviews, focus groups, etc. Any of these approaches can provide ideas and input to brainstorming sessions among staff (and perhaps a handful of regular users). They can then discuss all the ideas and rank and select those that may be worthy of further investigation.

In addition to direct consumer contact, reading the professional literature is an excellent avenue for appropriating marketing ideas that have been used successfully elsewhere.

Market Segments

The potential customers of a library are a fairly mixed group with a wide range of requirements. It is necessary to break this group down in order to identify segments or niches on which to concentrate. This breakdown should try to create groups with perceived common needs and can be done according to age, physical location, common interest, common work types, etc.

Specific groups may be all the senior managers in a company; all the 12– to16–year-olds in a public library context; all first-year psychology students, etc. Clearly, each group, known as a **market segment**, will want and expect something slightly different from the library, which, in turn, will have to develop a separate strategy for each group.

Competition

The competition faced by many libraries is not always obvious. However it does exist and has to be considered when developing longer-term strategies. With the advent of the Internet, free Wi-Fi in shopping centers and elsewhere, computer use at home, cheap photocopying, etc., consumers may feel they no longer need the library. Any initiative has to counter this competition by offering something different or adding value to a product.

Hence, the image of the library becomes most important. Perceptions must be managed. Is the library seen as a relevant, helpful, friendly, efficient place contributing to the well-being of its community? Try to build a high profile to assist with creating this perception. Become involved wherever possible and appropriate, and always build strong relations with the body that funds your activities.

Marketing Mix

'Marketing mix' emphasizes the need to provide an appropriate 'mix' when delivering a product or service to a specific market segment. Commonly referred to as the four Ps, the marketing mix considers:

- Product
- Price
- Place
- Promotion.

For instance, if you are dealing with top management in a special library or members of the library board for a public library, any service you provide to them will have to be of the highest quality in content and presentation, timely, and delivered in a fairly conservative manner. In providing a service to first-year undergraduates, the library will still have to be accurate but may present the service in a simpler manner; timeliness may be less critical; and innovative modes of presentation may be tried.

 EXERCISE 14.1

José works on his own in the small special library of a medium-sized company. He has decided to identify some specific market segments within the organization before he starts to determine their service needs—he feels this is the only way to approach his work. What variables might José consider to determine the composition of his groups?

Promotion

As noted above, any library or information service has to maintain a positive profile in order to continue and to expand its activities. Maintaining a positive profile is part of public relations and is a way of marketing the entire library to its community.

 Remember, you can't rely on word of mouth to build a positive image with users— customers are usually only vocal when things go wrong.

Before starting any promotional campaign, consider the following (adapted from Bangs and Halliday):

- which market segment is being targeted?—being specific will be more successful than a general campaign
- what are you trying to achieve?—e.g., promote a new service, increase patronage of an existing service, gain a new group of users
- when will the promotion be run and for how long?
- is a specific service to be promoted? What are its unique properties?
- where will the promotion be conducted?—e.g., the local shopping center, throughout the university, in the staff newsletter
- how will the promotion campaign be conducted?—e.g., using in-house expertise to develop materials such as a logo, slogan, etc., using prepared materials from a library organization, obtaining professional assistance, using existing staff or volunteers.

Of course, many of these decisions will be influenced by how much money and time are available.

A wide range of potential activities designed to ensure retention of existing users and attracting new users can be undertaken. These include:

- public relations
- advertising
- promotion and outreach.

Public Relations

- The online presence of your library is critical. For many it is the public face of the organization. Therefore attractive website design, easy navigation and importantly, regular updating are important factors in ensuring an eye-catching online presence.
- Exploiting social media—blogs, Twitter, wikis, Facebook etc.—offers opportunities but is also challenging. Maintaining a dynamic and attention grabbing presence isn't easy but is necessary if these tools are to work well for you.
- Physical presence is also important. Make the most of your space. Can you hold public events? Make it available to community groups? Provide meeting rooms, quiet areas, noisy areas? Make space for exhibitions featuring your material or that provided by others? Is its design warm and welcoming for all potential user groups?
- Produce regular news releases for local papers or in-house journals, and, for larger organizations, produce your own 'Library News' or equivalent. Invite the press to any or all events for which you can provide a 'story'. Build contacts with the local radio station and endeavour to gain air time on a regular basis.
- Provide articles for magazines, professional journals and conferences.
- For public libraries in particular, become involved in community activities at all levels.
- Be closely engaged with your funding body—local council, university administration, school management committee.

Advertising

- Advertising campaigns can be expensive so need to be carefully targeted. However, making the best use of social media is relatively free of direct costs (staff time is another matter!) and offers real opportunities to be creative and innovative.
- Try for sessions on local radio to announce initiatives—these will act as a form of advertising.
- Ensure that details of events are given to all media outlets. Become expert at writing press releases.
- Consider production of calendars, posters, fliers, bookmarks, etc. Maybe local design students can assist with these. Such items may also offer opportunities to attract sponsorship from local businesses or library materials suppliers to cover the cost of their production.

Promotion and Outreach

- An attractive web presence and a close relationship with the parent funding body are key overarching requirements for any promotional undertakings.
- Tie promotions or outreach activities in with anniversaries, special events, public holidays, etc.
- Put up posters, displays, etc. in public places. Become involved in community events and celebrations. Identify potential initiatives where the library can reach out to non-user groups.
- Depending on your library, visit classes, departments, staff meetings, seniors' groups, preschools, service clubs, etc. to promote your activities.
- Consider off-site delivery of workshops, hands-on training, etc.

EXERCISE 14.2

Maria is head librarian of a small public library system of three branches with a very limited budget. She would like to get more preschoolers into the libraries for story hour and other activities. Which promotional activities might Maria use in order to achieve her aim, and why?

SCENARIO

In a small group, consider the following case study as if you were the manager or supervisor. Use the discussion in this chapter as a guide and brainstorm other ideas and options. You are expected to deliver a practical and workable solution that is in the best interests of the staff and the organization.

Robin works for a major college library that has just been donated, on the death of a former college president, a large, well-organized collection of materials dealing with the history of the local area. She feels this is an important collection that should be made more widely known and, she hopes, used for research.

Discuss how Robin might develop a strategic marketing plan for the collection while at the same time managing to preserve and restrict access to more fragile and valuable materials.

References and Further Reading

American Library Association, *Advocating in a tough economy tool kit,* [online], 2012. http://www.ala.org/advocacy/advleg/advocacyuniversity/toolkit

American Library Association, *Citizens-save-libraries power guide,* [online], 2015. http://www.ala.org/united/powerguide

Bangs, David and Michael Halliday, *The Australian market planning guide,* 2nd ed., Warriewood, NSW, Australia, Woodslane, 2001.

Bly, Robert W., *The marketing plan handbook*, Madison, WI., Entreprenuer Press, 2009.

Feliciter (Journal of the Canadian Library Association), *Marketing libraries,* [special issue] 60:3, 2014.

FOCAL (Friends of Canadian Libraries), [online], 2015. www.friendsoflibraries.ca/

Germano, M.A., 'Narrative-based library marketing', *The Bottom Line* 23:1, 2010.

Lamb, Anette, *Marketing for libraries*, [online], 2014. http://eduscapes.com/marketing/index.htm

Ohio Library Council, *Marketing the library,* [online], 2008. http://olc.org/marketing/1intro.htm

Osif, Bonnie A., 'Branding, marketing and fund raising', *Library Administration and Management* 20:1, Winter 2006.

Reed, Sally Gardner, *Making the case for your library: a how-to-do-it manual for librarians,* New York, Neal-Schuman, 2001.

Walters, Suzanne, *Library marketing that works*, New York, Neal-Schuman, 2004.

CHAPTER FIFTEEN
Managing Change

Introduction

Change will occur throughout our lives, at home, at work, in the world around us, and in ourselves. We cannot prevent change from taking place. But we do have control over how we manage these changes.

 As a manager, it is your job to encourage positive change, to plan for it, to implement it, and to help staff accept and be enthusiastic supporters of it.

What is Change

Change can be seen as:

- ending a task, procedure, relationship, activity
- a transition period allowing adjustment, learning, coping, training
- embarking on a new activity, relationship, process.

Change can relate to:

- individuals—e.g., changing a problem behavior pattern (say, arriving at work late)
- tasks—e.g., the manner in which stack requests are completed and passed on to the stack attendant
- organizations—e.g., moving from free services to fee for service; reorganizing academic library services and information technology under a chief information officer; merging the National Library of Canada and the National Archives of Canada.

Each brings its own level of difficulty and demands different approaches. Changing individual work patterns or behavior relates closely to counseling and feedback and is covered in Chapter 10 of this book. This chapter concentrates on changing practices, procedures, and systems in the workplace.

Some change will be imposed by forces outside the organization's control; some will evolve through natural selection; some will be initiated by managers; and some will originate with staff. For change to be a positive experience for individuals and organizations, regardless of why it occurs, who initiated it, or whether it was sought or thrust upon the workplace, it is essential that it is properly managed.

Negotiation

Introducing change at any level requires negotiation with those staff affected by it. It is, therefore, important to understand how successful negotiating skills can be used in many situations. Negotiation involves consciously planning how to achieve your own ends while trying to meet the needs of others. It calls on both the research and human relations skills of a manager. In a work situation it should never be a win/lose process but one where both parties have something to gain by a successful outcome.

In order to meet these objectives, negotiators need to consider:
- the objective I am seeking and the other person's needs
- the pressures and concerns being felt by the other party
- focusing on issues, not people
- my bottom line—the minimum agreement I can accept; but also being flexible and willing to compromise
- maintaining calm and limiting emotion in discussions
- listening carefully to what is said and being aware of body language.

Objectives

Be clear about what you want to achieve before starting any negotiation. Is it the introduction of a new system you have already devised or is it that you just want a task done in a more efficient manner and want information on how this may be done? Being clear on objectives and spelling them out clearly to the participants will help to reduce the concerns and suspicions that the other parties may be harboring.

Pressures and Concerns

Establish as far as possible before any meetings what pressures and concerns may be felt. This will help considerably in understanding the other person's position and will assist in developing a solution that meets these concerns and your goals. A proper understanding of why he or she feels strongly about the issue is crucial to avoiding misunderstandings and limiting unhelpful argument.

The Issues, Not the Person

Maintain focus on the issue that is being discussed, and avoid being drawn into diversions relating to personalities. The latter can quickly lead to arguments and raised emotions, neither of which is conducive to a satisfactory outcome. While it is necessary to take into account how people will react and handle a situation (and thus how you will deal with it), do not let this become an issue in itself.

The Bottom Line

It is important to be clear in your own mind about your bottom line before starting the negotiation. However, also be aware that flexibility, consideration of new and creative solutions, dealing with concerns, and offering concessions will all help to achieve your ends. Be prepared to sell your solution by arguing the benefits of the preferred approach and demonstrating why it will be good for all parties.

Maintaining Calm
It is important to remain calm and present your position with logic and clarity. Separate the problem from the people and deal with issues and objectives—not feelings and positions. Care for what is being said and show your commitment to a successful outcome. Ensure, if agreement cannot be reached, that you have fully explained your position and what the next steps will be.

Here again, clarity will assist in avoiding misunderstanding and limiting emotional undertones that will be difficult to deal with and might cloud the real issues.

Listen and Observe
Always listen carefully to the other parties. Ask open-ended questions (why? what if? how?) in order to explore their attitudes and feelings and to avoid being defensive or arguing. Encourage them to talk, to explore options and ideas, and to be sure that you really do understand what is said—be prepared to summarize and recap as necessary. Watch body language to try and gauge if you have accurately assessed the situation—sometimes what is being said may not be what is felt. If deadlock appears to have been reached, take time out and then approach the situation from a different angle.

Why Negotiations Fail
Each negotiation is a unique process that may fail for a wide range of reasons. However, these can generally be summarized as:
- parties not addressing the fundamental issues involved
- parties not hearing what is said—their predetermined beliefs and attitudes prevent them listening effectively
- inflexibility—an unwillingness to see this as a two way process.

Always remember these points when entering into any negotiation and consider that both parties have goals, both have concerns, and hopefully, there is one best way that will address all of these needs.

EXERCISE 15.1

Consider how flexible and open to change you are. Below is a list of activities for you to undertake in the next few weeks. Look at each one and make a commitment to do it within the next month. If you feel uneasy about making this commitment, ask yourself why and note the reasons beside the activity. Revisit this list occasionally and repeat the exercise.

Get to work in a different way from normal (e.g., ask someone for a ride, catch the bus if you normally drive, or try a different route).

Volunteer to do something you would normally avoid.

Get to work 30 minutes earlier than usual.

Move your desk or, if that is not possible, rearrange the items on it.

Eat or drink something you have never tried before.

Sit down with at least one staff member each week and ask what one aspect they would change about their job if it could be done. Write down why this change can or cannot be implemented and discuss with the person concerned.

Ask somebody the question you have always wanted to ask them.

Make one contact in another organization with a colleague involved in similar work and swap ideas.

Look carefully at one work practice that has not changed for a while. Could it be improved?

Set yourself a goal for the week each Monday morning; on Friday, check whether it has been achieved.

Tackle a job, at home or at work, that you have been putting off for ages.

Make an effort to improve relations with the person in your area that you feel least connection with.

Planning for Change

A minor, temporary change will require far less managing than major change that will be permanent. However, all change requires consideration of the following in order to give it the best chance of success:

- have a clear understanding of why the change is necessary
- have clear, measurable aims and objectives as to what is to be achieved from the change. Be realistic as to what can or cannot be achieved
- consider how the success or failure of the change can be assessed against its aims
- develop a clear implementation plan and timetable for major change. Whenever possible, do not rush into changes, but allow time for staff and systems to adjust to the new practices or systems
- identify barriers and aids to implementation
- ensure that staff affected by the change are involved and consulted on the proposed change and the impact it may have
- try to involve key individuals or groups and to win their support as change agents
- be up-front and honest with everyone as to the anticipated impact of the change
- manage problems and concerns, be open to suggestions, and be ready to negotiate
- prepare training and regular feedback sessions as necessary
- ensure that timing is appropriate (e.g., the change is not introduced at the busiest time of the year)
- develop a suitable changeover or transition process
- allow sufficient time for the change and ensure that adequate resources are available to support its implementation
- when possible, consider implementing a pilot study
- monitor carefully the impact of the change in its initial stages.

Resistance to Change

Resisting change is common. Routine is an important part of most of our lives, and making changes can be difficult. We may be anxious about coping with the change, unsure of its impact, and worried about how long it will take to learn new tasks or implement the change.

Change can also bring about alterations in workgroups, individual status, or power structures that threaten a comfortable environment and challenge the individual's—or the group's—interests. For any manager, overcoming resistance to change will be critical. By using the previously mentioned techniques for implementing change, resistance should be minimized. In addition, depending upon the situation and the individuals concerned, the following strategies can assist in reducing resistance:

- ensure that change is introduced gradually
- listen carefully and negotiate fairly over staff concerns—be responsive to their ideas
- maximize communication opportunities—let everyone know exactly what is happening and encourage feedback through the entire process
- minimize unnecessary disruptions to staff by, for instance, having building work done after hours
- be positive and enthusiastic about the advantages the change will bring
- identify key staff members who will become 'change advocates', acting as role models who will influence other staff

- align the proposed changes with the individual's and organization's ethos and values
- maintain momentum and interest throughout the process
- try to ensure a successful change process—it makes the next one easier to implement.

Implementing Change

Taking the above points into consideration, it is possible to list steps that should be followed to assist in making the change orderly and effective and to minimize disruption and staff concerns. Note however that any change is likely at first to have a negative impact on productivity or service provision. Usually it takes time for new systems or practices to settle down. For staff and customers, it may take some readjusting to learn new skills or understand modified procedures.

Any substantial change process will therefore need time and patience to carry the process to a successful conclusion. Considering the following steps will assist in making the process go more smoothly:

1. *Involve staff* from the very beginning and ensure they understand the rationale behind the change and the benefits that will accrue. Make sure the change leadership team come from across the range of work places affected by the change and are committed to its implementation. Once staff understand what is being proposed, identify key staff who will become leaders or change agents in the process.

2. Meet and brainstorm with all staff to *identify problems and listen to concerns* regarding its impact. Be sure to have training and changeover processes clearly developed to present to staff.

3. *Assure staff that clients and users will be adequately informed* of the change process and its impact upon them. Be sure to consider, and acknowledge, the additional workload this may place on staff who may have to assist clients adjust to new systems.

4. If it is a major change, try to *introduce it in stages* and perhaps conduct a pilot phase to identify issues. Be sure to celebrate the completion of each stage and celebrate successes in order to maintain commitment and enthusiasm.

5. *Monitor progress* against the initial plan and have regular progress reviews where all staff involved can comment on the change, highlight problem areas, and try to pre-empt potential trouble.

6. *Have a final sign off* when the process has been completed and ensure that everyone involved has had adequate training and support in adjusting to the new system.

If these steps are followed, the process should proceed smoothly, despite any natural resistance to change or concerns over the nature of the new or altered systems.

For major change, these steps should be followed quite formally, with minutes taken of meetings, decisions broadcast widely, and a clear implementation plan and timetable developed. For less dramatic change, the steps should guide managers who may use them less formally, but who should still consider each step and its relevance in relation to the change proposed.

EXERCISE 15.2

Carmel works for the Government Archives, which occupies an old historic building about to undergo major extensions and renovations. These will take over a year to complete, resulting in major disruption to some of those working in the building.

Management has therefore decided to look for alternative accommodation for the departments most affected by the work. As the department head most affected, Carmel has been appointed the head of a small team looking at various office buildings that may be suitable. Using the following headings, consider some of the issues that may make staff cautious about the proposed change:

Location and transportation

Formal and informal relations with other staff

Facilities

Working conditions

Access to resources

Self-image, status

SCENARIO

In a small group, consider the following case study as if you were the manager or supervisor. Use the discussion in this chapter as a guide and brainstorm other ideas and options. You are expected to deliver a practical and workable solution that is in the best interests of the staff and the organization.

Belinda runs a highly successful special library in a federal government department. It is located close to a university campus and students come in regularly to use the materials in her library. They often ask staff for assistance and for online searching. Belinda doesn't mind these requests. As long as her main clients, the department's staff, get priority, she has no problem with helping the students. Students like using the library because of the direct relevance of its collection to their study, its convenient layout, and its helpful staff. One or two regulars who are doing postgraduate studies have commented to Belinda on how helpful the library has been and how useful they have found its resources.

Recently senior management have become aware of this situation and have told Belinda to develop and implement a policy by the start of next semester to charge students for the use of the library and its facilities—or to refuse them access. Belinda is very concerned about the impact of this change and how to bring it about.

Using the categories below, consider some of Belinda's concerns.

Effect on staff and students

What systems could be used to implement charges? How can the system be made fair?

How would you inform students of the charge?

How would you handle students used to the free service and reluctant to start paying?

Will this charge affect the quality of service delivered to students?

References and Further Reading

Craine, K., 'Managing the cycle of change', *Information Management Journal* 41:5, 2007.

Curzon, Susan Carol, *Managing change: a how-to-do-it manual for librarians*, New York, Neal-Schuman, 2006.

Fortune Group, *How to manage organisational change,* [online], 2015. http://www.fortunegroup.com.au/managing-change-in-the-workplace

Hamlin, Kristen, *How to implement change effectively*, [online]. http://www.ehow.com/how_2181271_implement-change-effectively.html

Lewis, David H., 'The innovator's dilemma: disruptive change and academic libraries', *Library Administration and Management* 18:2, Spring 2004.

Massey, Tinker, *Managing change and people in libraries*, Oxford, Chandos Publishing, 2009.

Soehner, Catherine B., 'Change management in libraries: An essential competency for leadership', *Proceedings of the IATUL Conference*, 2014, [online], http://docs.lib.purdue.edu/cgi/viewcontent.cgi?article=2059&context=iatul

CHAPTER SIXTEEN
Security Issues

Introduction

Managers face a number of security issues in their day-to-day work. In libraries and information centers the major security concerns relate to staff, users, resources, and the building. It is an essential part of the manager's job to minimize risks and to prevent accidental and deliberate breaches of security (rather than have to act after the event).

Security in this context covers the whole area of physical care. It is concerned with ensuring that material is not stolen; it is also concerned with ensuring that staff or members of the public are not hurt in the building. In any changes to job or building design, safety and security issues will be major concerns.

Proper systems and procedures need to be in place to limit, as far as possible, the likelihood of security problems arising, and to deal with situations that may occur. Safety of people is of paramount concern, and the systems and procedures must reflect this priority. Apart from the obvious ethical issues relating to a safe workplace, injured staff impose a heavy financial burden on the organization through workers' compensation claims and lost productivity.

Staff

Issues relating to staff are varied and cover the spectrum from problems that may affect staff to staff members themselves being the problem. Basic occupational safety and health requirements are covered in Chapter 9 of this book. This section will look at these issues from a broader perspective, the main areas being:

- job design
- workplace
- training
- equipment.

Job Design

Jobs must be properly designed, lest they cause harm to the staff member performing the task. Prolonged use of computer equipment requires that care be taken in the design of workstations and equipment and to ensure that regular breaks are taken. Workloads must be reasonable and actions that may increase stress avoided. Regular occupational safety and health inspections of the workplace should be undertaken by a suitably trained person; any problems identified should be dealt with promptly.

Job design also applies to employees working from home and special care must be taken to ensure that any staff members doing work from home fully understand their responsibilities to maintain a safe working environment. In such circumstances it may be advisable to get professional advice before agreeing to home-based working for any staff member.

Workplace

The workplace itself can cause difficulties which cannot always be readily resolved. Old buildings, designed in an earlier era, may be insufficiently supplied with electrical outlets— leading to extension cords and power boards being used—or have steep flights of stairs which may have to be negotiated while carrying books or other materials.

While changing the physical fabric of the workplace may take time, money and planning there can sometimes be simpler remedies for problems.

 For example,

- a circulation or information desk near drafty front doors can be moved slightly, or the doorway changed
- a library's public spaces can be re-arranged to use them more efficiently, allowing high stack shelves to be lowered.

Training

Staff training is important in minimizing security breaches and accident risks. New staff members in particular need to become familiar with security procedures. They should be made aware of regulations regarding, for example, the use of work vehicles and of proper manual work practices such as lifting. It is quite common to require new staff sign a form acknowledging that they have been instructed in the security and safety aspects of their work (see Chapter 10). Note that any supervisor is responsible to ensure that staff have adequate training in order to undertake the job. If this is not provided, and an employee injures themselves trying to do the task, the supervisor or the employer may be liable.

Equipment

Proper equipment, like training, plays an important role in maximizing security and minimizing accidents. Well-designed air conditioning systems improve conditions for staff and materials; well-designed theft-detection systems limit the loss of material; and suitable shelving or packaging protect the collection.

Users

Clients using any facility should be protected by the provision of a reasonable level of safety and security. The managers of an area owe a duty of care to anyone in that area. If it is shown that they were negligent (i.e., did not use the common sense that an 'average' person would expect), then they or their organization may be liable for damages. Thus users should expect

- a safe environment
- appropriate systems
- accommodation of differences.

A Safe Environment

A safe and properly designed environment is suitable for the purpose for which it is intended. Examples include a well-lit parking garage to ensure the safety of patrons leaving at night; front doors that are not too heavy for elderly patrons to open; non-slip floors and steps; no loose electrical cords or ragged carpets.

Appropriate Systems

Appropriate systems help ensure the safety of users who may not be familiar with the building, the fittings and equipment, or ways of accessing the material. Proper signage is essential (particularly noting exits); restricted access areas must be clearly marked; equipment such as photocopiers or computers must be regularly serviced to ensure their safety as well as functioning; etc.

Accommodation of Differences

Users come in all shapes and sizes, and this diversity has to be taken into account, whether in terms of shelves and counter height, access for the disabled, positioning of electrical equipment (such as computers) so that young children will not have unsupervised access to them, and so on.

EXERCISE 16.1

Jean is the supervisor of the city government's general information help desk. This is a busy facility, helping residents with inquiries about taxes, building permits, public housing, dog licenses, etc. It is housed in an old building that is very cramped and has limited access up a steep flight of steps. Money is available for redesigning the building internally (the outside is protected by a historic-district ordinance) and Jean has been asked to prepare a proposal on any improvements that can be made to the help desk. Using the headings below, consider some of the changes Jean might propose.

A safe environment

Appropriate systems

Accommodation of differences

Collections

For all libraries and information centers, their collections (whether books, paper files, documents, plans, correspondence, or computer files) are of paramount importance. Maintaining their safety and integrity should be a primary concern for all staff. Management has to establish practices and procedures that ensure, as far as possible, that its collection is accessible to its users but also protected from loss or damage. These aims often conflict, and a balance has to be achieved between the extremes of perfect safety and wide-open access.

The issues to be considered are:
- deliberate theft or damage
- environmental risks
- collection management.

Deliberate Theft or Damage

Theft or deliberate damage of collection items is unfortunately a fact of life for many institutions. 'High risk' materials such as rare, valuable, controversial, or particularly appealing items need to be covered by systems that include:
- supervised and/or limited access
- checking items after they have been borrowed and returned
- restrictions on lending
- high-level security tagging systems to prevent unauthorized removal
- regular physical checks.

Management must accept, and budget for, the inevitable damage and loss that will occur, despite proper security measures.

Environmental Risks

Risks caused by degradation, loss, or accidental damage often cause more problems to the collection than deliberate acts of vandalism. Water damage after heavy rain, high humidity in hot climates with subsequent mold growth, and insect or rodent damage can all be prevented with care and proper systems. Loss may be reduced by regular inventory and more sophisticated security systems. Accidental damage may be reduced by forms of protection such as packaging (e.g., covering books, boxing files and pamphlets, etc.) and providing clear instructions on how to use items (e.g., directing output to a printer).

Collection Management

The collection is also placed at risk by poor management practices, including inappropriate collection decisions resulting in large amounts of little-used material, poor shelving practices, and infrequent weeding. Related problems result from the extensive use of computers for storing and accessing information. Problems with individual PCs can generally be overcome with little difficulty, but if an entire network goes down, leaving no functioning computer in the library, it is a far more difficult situation. Fortunately this sort of occurrence is rare, but a contingency plan needs to be in place to ensure that, to some degree, services can be continued and customers not too badly inconvenienced. In addition, a proper backup schedule of all files, with recovery procedures that are regularly checked to ensure they work, is fundamental to the design of any computer system.

Buildings

If the collection is to remain secure and staff and users protected, the building fabric itself must be safe and functional. Whether a building is being planned or already exists, similar concerns must be considered:

- weatherproof design
- infrastructure
- emergency procedures.

Weatherproof Design

How weatherproof is the building? Is the external fabric keeping out extremes of weather such as heavy rain or hot summer sun (which will cause rapid deterioration of paper-based collections)? Part of a manager's job is to examine, in general terms, the outside of the building at least once a week (and immediately after weather extremes) to ensure that all is functioning as it should.

Infrastructure

Regular maintenance and repair of infrastructure is also important. Electrical cables, especially extension cords, should not run across floors; Wi-Fi connectivity should be appropriate to the demand; lighting and heating/cooling systems should function properly; shelving should be secure; access to fire extinguishers should not be hampered; etc. Again, managers should inspect their areas regularly to ensure that problems have not gone unnoticed.

Emergency Procedures

Fire drills and emergency evacuation procedures must be undertaken on a regular basis and proper signage posted in all areas. Ensuring that these drills are carried out is not always easy. Staff are usually busy; it creates disturbance; and it can frequently be seen as a waste of time. It is necessary to overcome this attitude by emphasizing the importance of the drills, setting a good example, and making them part of a regular routine. Up-to-date lists of staff and emergency contact telephone numbers should be maintained and prominently displayed.

EXERCISE 16.2

Following a heavy storm one afternoon, the gutters of the Downtown Public Library overflowed and caused a considerable amount of water to come through the roof and down one wall. Fortunately, little of the collection was damaged, but the leaks left quite a mess. A subsequent investigation showed that an empty potato chip bag had blown across the roof and gotten stuck against the overflow drain on the roof, causing the backup problem.

The library director is upset, and wants to know what you, as the branch manager, are going to do about it.

Disaster Prevention

Disasters are usually preventable with planning and proper procedures. It is the manager's responsibility to ensure that such planning has been done, appropriate procedures developed and staff training undertaken.

With policies and procedures in place, it is important to get into detail when developing a disaster management plan. At such times, having straightforward, readily available information at hand can be vital in helping to ensure an emergency does not become a disaster.

Howell (1994, p. 28), in describing an actual emergency situation, noted the importance of the following information:

- the addresses and phone numbers of all areas covered by the plan
- where building plans, insurance policies, and other valuable records are stored
- the telephone numbers of key individuals to be contacted in an emergency. These will include staff as well as the emergency services, and must be kept up to date. A 'telephone tree' may also be useful for showing who is to call whom next
- clear identification of who can talk to the media
- a list of local suppliers, including companies, that can provide emergency equipment or supplies
- specific materials that are most valuable and thus need the greatest attention in a general emergency
- basic salvage steps for dealing with particular media, e.g., paper files, posters, or actual equipment – photocopiers, PCs.

All of the above is vital information but it is no use if buried in a lengthy, nicely bound disaster management plan. The key information should be summarized on one sheet of paper, distributed widely, and readily available. In an emergency the last thing you want to do is run around looking for the disaster manual. There are a number of templates and examples readily available on the Internet and it is useful to check these out and tailor one according to your own specific requirements.

Note that today, IT infrastructure is critical in virtually all organizations and specific disaster plans need to be in place focused on this, supported by appropriate policies and procedures.

Developing a plan requires commitment and time. It may be useful to use an outside consultant. Borrowing someone else's plan may also provide guidance. Using some of the references below or searching the Internet will also offer guidance. But in the end, you have to develop a unique plan for your own situation and it will take a modest amount of time and effort. Once a procedure is put in place and maintained, a manager will feel less exposed if disaster does happen. With thoughtful planning and evaluation, the likelihood of emergencies developing into disasters will be lessened appreciably.

SCENARIO

In a small group, consider the following case study as if you were the manager or supervisor. Use the discussion in this chapter as a guide and brainstorm other ideas and options. You are expected to deliver a practical and workable solution that is in the best interests of the staff and the organization.

Jasmine is overseeing the redevelopment and modernization of her public library. The work being done is quite extensive—walls will be pulled down and re-erected, carpet replaced, shelving replaced, new power points and lighting installed, a wheelchair accessible rest room built and the entrance completely remodeled. The work is expected to take eight weeks and during this time the library will remain open and continue to provide, as far as possible, 'business as usual'.

Jasmine has been asked by her local government body to provide an outline of some of the safety and security issues that need to be considered—and planned for— before the contractor starts work.

Think about the points she might raise under the following headings:

Challenges for staff

Challenges for users

Challenges for collection material

Challenges related to the external environment (e.g. bad weather, builders causing disruption etc.)

References and Further Reading

Australian Library and Information Association (ALIA), *ALIA disaster planning for libraries*, [online], 2010.
https://www.alia.org.au/sites/default/files/documents/ALIA_Disaster_Planning_Libsfinal.pdf

Brodie, Lynn, *Emergency preparedness planning for library collections: Development of a program and lessons learned*, [online], 2012.
http://conference.ifla.org/past-wlic/2012/200-brodie-en.pdf

Hoover Institution Library and Archives, *Disaster preparedness plan*, [online],
http://web.stanford.edu/~rayan/preservation/disasterplanvendors.pdf

Howell, Allan G., 'What a disaster', *New Librarian* May 1994.

Jones, Virginia A. & Kris E. Keyes, *Management wise: how to develop an emergency management plan*, [online], 2008.
http://content.arma.org/IMM/MarchApril2008/how_to_develop_an_emergency_management_plan.aspx

Matthews, Graham, Yvonne Smith & Gemma Knowles, *Disaster management in archives, libraries and museums*, Farnham, Surey, Ashgate, 2009.

Northeast Document Conservation Center, *Collections security: Planning and prevention for libraries and archives*, [online].
https://www.nedcc.org/free-resources/preservation-leaflets/3.-emergency-management/3.11-collections-security-planning-and-prevention-for-libraries-and-archives

Robertson, Guy, *Disaster planning for libraries: process and guidelines*, London, Chandos, 2015.

CHAPTER SEVENTEEN
Managing Self

Introduction
In order to succeed in managing others, managers and supervisors need a clear awareness of their own strengths and weaknesses, managerial style, motivational factors, personal goals, and career objectives. Insight into these areas will help in the day-to-day implementation of policy and procedure and assist in relationships with staff and other managers.

Self-awareness is an important asset for a manager. Without it the possibility of change and improvement in management style and approach are unlikely. In effect, the ability to manage oneself is just as necessary as the ability to manage others.

Understanding Personal Strengths and Weaknesses
Knowing one's areas of strength and weakness will assist in developing a satisfying and rewarding work and personal life. Everyone has strengths and weaknesses. Successful managers know their own strong points and limitations and get to know the strengths and weaknesses of their staff.

 The basic aim is to maximize strengths, minimize weaknesses.

Using this awareness, managers can try to involve staff in work that appeals to their strengths and capabilities and avoids their weaknesses. This will not always be possible but should certainly be considered when building teams and assigning tasks that require a mix of talents.

Identifying individual strengths and weaknesses takes time working with people. As well as personal observation, tools have been developed to assist in identifying individual strengths and weaknesses, traits, and behavior preferences. These tools are usually applied under supervision and the results determined by a qualified and experienced person.

 Examples include:
- the Margerison-McCann Team Management Systems Development International (TMSDI), a set of questions, completed by individuals, which indicate their work style preferences
- the Myers-Briggs Type Indicator (MBTI), a set of questions designed to identify individual preferences and biases in the way people make decisions.

Because everyone is different, with beliefs, backgrounds, perceptions, and reactions that vary hugely, managers have to cope with a wide range of behaviors. Some will be a strength in certain situations, others weaknesses. Awareness of your strengths and an understanding of your weaker areas are important assets.

Managing Stress

Stress is felt by everyone. It may be caused by pressures at work, at home, or a combination of the two. While a certain level of stress is virtually inevitable for most people, minimizing it is important in order to ensure that it does not become dysfunctional. Controlling work-related stress is a joint responsibility shared by you and your manager and a number of simple approaches can assist.

Thus, for managers:

- give staff autonomy and control over their work—the more they are in control of things the more comfortable they should feel
- ensure staff have the requisite skills and knowledge to undertake the work (or have training provided)
- as far as possible, provide job security and career development
- create a supportive, friendly work environment—lead by example in establishing this
- ensure that the physical working environment is as good as possible and do take staff concerns seriously when they raise any related issues
- make certain expected targets and work performance expectations are reasonable and that these standards have been established after discussion with staff
- when introducing new practices and procedures, even minor changes, ensure that staff are involved in the implementation, that they are properly trained, and that time is allowed for the process to be properly established
- as a manager be approachable, prepared to listen carefully to individual concerns and to keep any such discussions confidential. While you are not (usually) a trained counsellor, you should be able to listen empathically and direct staff to an appropriate service if their concerns relate to their non-work life.

For yourself, the following tips may help:

- set realistic expectations—daily and longer term
- focus on successes rather than failures
- when things go wrong, ask yourself will anybody remember, or care, in a year's time?—though also think about what went wrong and learn from the experience
- remember that life can be difficult—everyone has to cope with things that do not run smoothly
- take periodic breaks from what you are doing—reflect, reward yourself, and spend a few minutes on something quite different
- use 'to do' lists to help in completing tasks
- break big jobs into smaller, manageable chunks with clear completion points
- quite often you can't control what goes on around you, e.g., a difficult supervisor, but you can control the way you react—do not let others dictate your well-being
- do regular physical exercise of any sort and if possible, when really stressed, go for a walk or other physical exercise—you will feel better. Remember, maintaining physical and emotional well-being is your responsibility and under your control—do not let external events and other people control how you feel.

Time Management

Time management is a perennial problem. Below are some basic strategies, which should be adjusted to suit your situation. Personal time management is essential for managers, as is the ability to encourage others in positive time-management practices.

Countless books have been written on the subject, and professionals give regular lectures and training sessions. It is well worth getting a book or attending a lecture. However, there are a number of common tips or strategies that are relevant to most work situations:

- Firstly, *maintain a 'time diary'* for a typical work week where you record what you are doing say every 15 minutes (you can download a template readily from the Internet). This can help highlight how much of your time is spent on doing what you had planned, and how much not. Typically, you may find 50% of your time is spent on reacting, and is not focused on your planned objectives. Being aware of this can provide the impetus to get serious about how you manage your time and stick to your priorities.
- *Set out a weekly schedule* where you block out time for planning and other key tasks. Ensure this is readily available—stick it up on your wall, have it widely accessible via your diary software. This lets everyone know that some times are off limits except for emergencies. At the same time, maintain a daily 'to do' list, diary, or organizer that you write up first thing every morning and check off at the end of the day. Include short, simple actions and break large tasks down into small, manageable chunks.
- *Prioritize tasks and break them into groups.* Always do the important and urgent right away and ask yourself what is the worst that can happen if the urgent (but not important) is left. For most people, the morning is the time we are at our most alert so tackle those challenging tasks first, ahead of the rest. Do not start lots of jobs at the same time and as far as possible, follow the maxim of 'handling the paper once only', i.e., start the job and finish it in one process.
- *Do it now.* Set objectives, be strict in achieving them, and reward yourself—e.g., take a coffee break, rest and relax, take a short walk away from the workplace, etc.
- *Delegation* can be difficult but is important. Think about what can be delegated and make sure you can truly let go the task. Then prioritize staff training to ensure delegation is successful. Commitment of time on this now will pay dividends later.
- *Oppose unrealistic deadlines* and be honest when setting them with others.
- *Learn to say no* without offending—usually other staff will appreciate and value your honesty. Remember, no one can do everything.
- Try to *limit drop-in visitors*—e.g., by standing when they arrive, not having a visitor's chair near your desk, etc. Learn to terminate meetings once the issue has been addressed.
- *Try not to react immediately to everything that comes up*—maybe it will sort itself out in time. This particularly relates to managing your email. Decide when you will look at your email and be strict. Turn off the email 'received' alert in order to reduce the temptation!
- Set in place systems and procedures that *streamline work and provide milestones* against which progress can be measured.
- *Schedule meetings* near lunchtime or toward the end of the day to help ensure they do not run too long. Always set agendas for meetings and aim to stick to them.

Working with People and Helping Yourself

One of the main attributes of a successful manager is the ability to work with people. Maintaining good relations with your staff, with senior managers to whom you are accountable, and with internal and external colleagues requires a conscientious effort. The following strategies may be helpful:

- active listening
- networking
- belonging to professional organizations
- working with your boss.

Active Listening

Use active listening to improve your ability to communicate and form relationships with others. Give the person you are talking to your undivided attention, and make this clear by maintaining eye contact, paraphrasing and reflecting their comments and concerns, summarizing occasionally, and asking open-ended questions to stimulate further discussion. Essentially, active listening requires you to show your concern for others and to forget your own needs for that period. It is a powerful tool that builds respect and positive feelings, leading to increased confidence and success in dealing with situations and improved relationships.

Networking

Network actively within and outside your organization. Networking involves making an effort to establish—and maintain—contacts with others who may be useful in your job or career. It should be done at work as a matter of course, and at conferences, courses, and meetings when you can. The wider your circle of contacts, the more information is shared and the more unforeseen opportunities arise. In addition, being seen and known within your organization or profession will help build a positive image of yourself with other managers and staff. After all, staff want to work for a manager who is respected and seen as successful.

Belonging to Professional Organizations

As part of networking, become involved in an appropriate professional organization. Be actively involved and volunteer for jobs or positions, write papers, go to conferences, etc. Valuable contacts are made in this way and, again, a positive image is created of someone dedicated to their profession and willing to put effort into it.

Working with Your Boss

Get along with your boss! This should be done by gaining an understanding of his or her pressures and priorities, work style, and strengths and weaknesses. Find out what is expected of you, be loyal, and help your boss succeed. Do high-quality work and be positive and solution oriented in problem situations. If you help your manager to succeed you will also be successful, and the rewards will flow to all staff.

EXERCISE 17.1

Using the headings below, spend a few minutes considering what steps you can take in the next week to actively improve some work relationships. Set yourself the goal of taking one step each week for the next five weeks.

Use active listening to improve a relationship

Network internally

Network externally

Find out more about a relevant professional organization

Take one action aimed at raising your profile with your manager or supervisor

Ethics

Because managers and supervisors exercise power and influence, they need a clear understanding of what constitutes ethical behavior in the workplace. Unfortunately, what appears to be a correct approach to one individual may seem totally unethical to another. This divergence arises from a mix of personal characteristics and experience, and the organizational culture that prescribes what is regarded as right or wrong behavior.

However, regardless of the 'grey' nature of what is ethical behavior, managers have a duty to try to reduce ambiguity and ensure that staff are clear about what is and is not acceptable. Organizations often draw up codes of ethics that new employees must read and agree to; standards of conduct are explained to new staff, and in certain circumstances where there is potential for difficult or conflict situations to arise, training in what constitutes an ethical approach to these situations may be put in place.

Setting a clear example of ethical behavior helps to shape an ethical organizational culture. Emphasizing its importance and encouraging staff to discuss any problems is a positive approach toward building an appropriate working environment that will be equitable for staff and users.

EXERCISE 17.2

Consider the issues raised in the following situations. What would you do? Why?

1. You work in a library that is disposing of its holdings of old LP records. While boxing them up to go to the Friends of the Library for sale, you notice an early Beatles record that you think may have a value of around $100, but that you expect the Friends will sell for only a dollar or two. As a Beatles fan yourself, you would like to take the record home to add to your collection (no one would ever know) and you have no intention of selling it.

2. You work for the local chamber of commerce. Your funds have been cut severely this year and you have been told to lay off two temporary staff and replace them with volunteers who (you are told) will be easy to find. You have been told explicitly that services are not to be cut to fit the reduced budget.

3. Your library spends $10,000 a year with one journal supplier and has done so for many years. In talking with their representative, you happen to mention that a particular art magazine you read at home (and which the library does not subscribe to) has become too expensive at $50 a month, and that you are going to stop getting it. The representative offers to arrange a 'free' subscription for you—a favor for a friend, he calls it.

4. You are the supervisor of a small team in a large office. You have been going out with a more junior staff member, Linda, who works for another supervisor in the same office. No one else knows of the relationship and you want to keep it that way. An opportunity arises for someone to work for a short period on your team. Linda's supervisor suggests she would be the right person for the position and deserves the opportunity. This would make you her direct supervisor.

GOAL -SETTING EXERCISE
(Based on an exercise developed by Kolb, Rubin, and McIntyre)
This is an individual exercise that should take around 90 minutes. Be prepared to discuss aspects of your goal-setting program with the group.

Personal Achievement Work Plan
Step 1
List briefly as many goals as you can think of that you wish to achieve within the next two years.
(Spend 10 minutes on this.)

Step 2

Select three of the most important goals from your list (career or personal), describe them in more detail, and rank them in order of importance. Note whether each goal will be difficult, moderately difficult, or easy to achieve. Also, alongside each goal note briefly how you will feel once the goal is achieved and what effect it will have on your life. (20 minutes)

1.

2.

3.

Step 3

Set up a matrix with goals 1, 2, and 3 across the top and down the sides. The aim is to establish whether working toward the attainment of one will make it more difficult to achieve another. Thus if one goal conflicts with another, write 'X' in the appropriate square of the matrix; if it has no effect, write 'O'; if it is a positive help, write '+' in the square. (10 minutes)

Example

	Goal 1 (Overseas trip)	Goal 2 (New kitchen)	Goal 3 (Have a baby)
Goal 1 (Overseas trip)		X	X
Goal 2 (New kitchen)	X		O
Goal 3 (Have a baby)	X	O	

As you can see, going overseas and building a new kitchen conflict, as each will take a lot of money.

Having a baby will make it more difficult to go overseas but probably won't have much impact on getting a new kitchen.

Your Matrix

	Goal 1	Goal 2	Goal 3
Goal 1			
Goal 2			
Goal 3			

Step 4

From the three goals, select one that you wish to start working on now and that will not be in conflict with another goal you may wish to pursue in the short term.

> **Your Goal:**

For this goal it is important to have a clear understanding of what you are hoping to achieve. Therefore, undertake the following (20 minutes):

State as explicitly as possible exactly how much of the goal you want to achieve in the next six months.

Spell out clearly how important it is to you that you achieve this much of the goal.

Expand on how you will feel in six months when this much of the goal is achieved.

Write down how you will feel if you do not achieve it.

What do you think are your chances of succeeding and what will have changed if you do succeed?

What will happen if you fail?

Step 5

List the obstacles that can keep you from reaching your goals. Include personal shortcomings as well as things outside your control. Beside each obstacle note anything you can do to overcome it. (20 minutes)

Step 6

List who can help you achieve your goal, what they can do, and what you will ask specifically of them. (10 minutes)

Step 7

List the specific tasks you are going to undertake over the next six months toward achieving your goal.

Beside each task note the date by which it will be completed. Make sure these are 'bite-size' tasks with a timeframe no longer than two weeks for completion. (20 minutes)

Step 8
Give a copy of the task list to someone important in your life. Ask them to follow up on the deadlines and seek regular feedback from you on progress toward your goal. Impress upon them the importance of their role in ensuring your success.

 Achieving most goals can be surprisingly easy and extremely satisfying. You must be clear what the goal is; know how you will achieve it; break it into small, manageable tasks; set sensible, realistic deadlines; and be disciplined about meeting them.

📖 References and Further Reading

Boyd, Melanie, 'Juanita's paintings: a manager's personal ethics and performance review', *Library Administration and Management* 19:1, Winter 2005.

Chapman, Alan, *Time management techniques and systems,* [online], 2015. http://www.businessballs.com/timemanagement.htm

Flanagan, Neil & Jarvis Finger, *Managing yourself and your career*, Sydney, Woodslane, 2013.

Goleman, Daniel, *Working with emotional intelligence*, New York, Bantam Books, 2000.

Hines, Samantha, *Productivity for librarians: how to get more done in less time*, Oxford, Chandos, 2010.

International Federation of Library Associations (IFLA), *Code of ethics for librarians and other information workers*, [online], 2012. http://www.ifla.org/news/ifla-code-of-ethics-for-librarians-and-other-information-workers-full-version

Kolb, David A., Irwin M. Rubin and James M. McIntyre, *Organizational psychology: an experiential approach*, Englewood Cliffs, N.J., Prentice-Hall, 1984.

MacKenzie, Alec & Pat Nickerson, *The time trap*, 4th ed., New York, American Management Association, 2009.

Mindtools, *Essential skills for an excellent career*, [online], 2015. www.mindtools.com/

Newlen, Robert, *Resume writing and interview techniques that work: a how-to-do-it manual for librarians*, New York, Neal-Schuman, 2006.

Schilling, Dianne, *10 steps to effective listening*, [online], 2012. http://www.forbes.com/sites/womensmedia/2012/11/09/10-steps-to-effective-listening/

Schinnerer, John L., *Guide to self: the beginner's guide to managing emotion and thought*, Bloomington, Ind., AuthorHouse, 2007.

Shepell, *Workhealthlife*, [online], 2015. https://www.workhealthlife.com/

ANSWERS

All the suggested answers are, by the nature of the questions and the subject itself, only possibilities and guides, not necessarily the right answer. Try to use these answers as a guide to stimulate your own thoughts if you are stuck on an exercise.

Answers are not included for case studies and for exercises where each response is likely to be different—e.g., personal response, individual library structure.

EXERCISE 1.1
Liz needs to think about:

Planning	Clarifying the availability of staff for particular times and duties The actual timetable/schedule Staff recruitment if necessary Changes in work practices and procedures that may be necessary Budget implications and how to manage them long-term
Organizing	Whether money is available to meet the costs Whether enough suitable staff are available Whether appropriate systems are in place
Leading	Setting an example by working some evenings on the desk Being available to meet and discuss staff concerns Explaining the reasons for the change Enthusiastically implementing the change, 'selling' it to staff
Controlling	Putting review processes in place to see how it is working out Monitoring budget expenditure Encouraging staff and user feedback

EXERCISE 1.2
Liz will probably need to concentrate on:

Human skills	Exercising skills to meet staff concerns about the change Keeping the balance between temps and permanents Ensuring that staff members are not stressed and have the requisite skills
Technical skills	Budgeting skills Scheduling skills Understanding how circulation, reference duties, etc. can be balanced
Conceptual skills	Considering how long-term planning may impact on the system Considering how long-term changes in the area may affect demand

EXERCISE 1.3

University librarian	Long-term growth
	Budgeting over the next five years, including fundraising and related issues
	Access and accommodation
	Relations with the rest of the university
	Technological change
Middle management	Coping with increased demand and less stable staffing
	Developing smarter ways of doing things—getting more out of staff
	Need for ongoing staff training and development
	Fewer permanents, more temps
Front-line supervisors	Concerns over job security; maintaining morale
	Increasingly demanding user base
	Expanding resources available, e.g., the Web
	Doing more with less

EXERCISE 2.1

Some issues facing a public library, for instance, may include:

Government policies	Fee-for-service principles being forced on organizations
	Reduced funding base for government, reduced funding for library
	Closure of other related government services
	Introduction of a sales tax on books, journals, etc.
Social values	Need to update the collection more often
	Demand for DVDs, ebooks, computer software
	Vocal and demanding pressure groups
Demographics and Geography	Aging local population
	Closure of local school library
	Changing ethnic makeup
Tradition	Employing a children's librarian—can it still be justified?
	Subscribing to certain daily newspapers
	Journals can only be read in the library
The market	A youth center opens across the street
	A link is developed with local preschools
	Library offers an information service to local businesses
Changes in technology	Introduction of a digital repository package
	Clients expect high speed Wi-Fi throughout the library
	Newspapers and other resources available online
Competitors	Free Wi-Fi at next door coffee shop
	New discount bookstore opens
	Expansion of local school library
	Commercial Internet access providers, Internet cafes etc.

Suppliers	Serial suppliers increase charges significantly
	Building maintenance contract outsourced and help no longer as available

EXERCISE 2.2

The Digital Library Federation may have to consider (strategies taken from the DLF website):

Opportunities	Increased access to collections possible via the Web
	Increased interest in digital self-publication within academe
	Widespread adoption of Z39.50 standards
	Success of the JSTOR journal preservation project
	Availability of foundation grant money
Threats	Low awareness of the need for digital preservation
	Rapidly changing technologies
	Diversity of local practices and standards for digitization
Strategies	Design and develop local digitization projects to produce digital surrogates for analog information objects
	Design and develop data-creation projects that produce 'born digital' information resources
	Select existing third-party data resources for inclusion in a collection
	Develop Internet gateways comprising locally maintained pages or databases of Web links to third-party networked information

EXERCISE 3.1

Some of the things Stephanie has to consider:

Policies, etc.	Opening hours of the center and staff scheduling
	Relationship with city government
	Staff involvement in planning for the future
	Volunteer vs. permanent staff and the allocation of work, shifts, etc.
Structure	Part of a bigger organization, e.g., city government
	Hierarchy and organizational design—can permanent staff move into other government departments?
	Is there a division of tasks at the center?
Nature of service	Providing basic handouts, advice, etc.
	Monotony of some work
	Possibility of unhappy clients
	More complex work (e.g., promotion program) and involvement of volunteers
	The status associated with the various types of work
Management style	Authoritative vs. democratic
	Differences in managing permanents and volunteers
Technology	Link to governmental systems?
	Access to information services such as the Internet
	Who uses the technology, provides training, etc.

Budget	What is the split of dollars between resources and staff? Is there any attempt to cost out activities or earn income?
Other	Amount of authority given to staff Team membership (i.e., who works with whom)

EXERCISE 3.2

Kerrie will need to work on

Tradition	The tradition of teachers having access to new books will be hard to break. Kerrie will need to do a lot of planning and preparation before making any change here.
Personal needs	Teaching staff will argue that they have a need for the material. Kerrie will have to try to counteract this by offering alternatives.
Bureaucracy	This should not be a major issue in this situation.
Charismatic leaders	If a strong informal leader among the staff is against any change, it will be more difficult for Kerrie to implement. She needs to work on these people first to try to win them over.

EXERCISE 5.2

Patrick may have to deal with

Inability to set goals	If no goals currently exist, establishing new ones may be difficult as employees may be unsure, except in very general terms, what is to be achieved. Lack of senior management support. Not wishing to write down the goals—employees understand what they want, and that's enough. Fear that failure will be more obvious if the goals are written down.
Resistance to change	The current system may be seen by workers as OK. Concern over the training load that may be required. Concern over when/how to implement the change and the extra work it will involve.
Time constraints	In a busy office, the time taken to plan and implement this change, together with the cost, may make it appear impractical.
Qualitative measures	The new system will deal primarily with numbers and accounts—how can it help measure the quality of work? What control measures can be introduced to help?
Unforeseen changes	Will the new system cope with proposed changes? What about staff turnover and training load? Will the amount of work done now be the same in three years' time?

EXERCISE 6.1

In order to meet their desire to benefit the economy and enriching cultural life, the British Library may develop strategic plans focusing on:

- How to engage with the commercial sector of the UK economy and develop services focused on helping them meet their needs
- Focus in on special libraries within corporations in order to provide training, resources and support for them to grow in their roles within such organizations
- Develop a regular travelling exhibition program of world class materials from its collection in order to reach major population centers throughout the UK
- Encourage public participation in the development of mash-ups or curated exhibitions drawn from the Library's digital holdings.

EXERCISE 6.2

The mission statement might be along the lines of the following:

> The Consort Ebook Agency will provide access to the largest range of ebooks, and formats, possible while offering the greatest flexibility in licensing arrangements attractive to all libraries, big and small, as well as to major consortia. Our aim is to be the leading provider of ebooks to university and public libraries in this country within the next five years.

Strategies may include:

- Simplified licensing agreements that are easy to understand and highly flexible
- Promotional campaigns at ALA conferences and elsewhere to raise visibility for the company
- Aggressive negotiations with ebook publishers aimed at acquiring exclusive distribution rights

EXERCISE 7.1

Nikhil would probably be worried about:

Involvement in the decision	Were his concerns about stress taken seriously? Job security Job design and work flow
Technology	How the accounting system will work if someone decides to pay for further consultation—how does he time them, who will invoice them, etc.? Will he need changes to the computer software he currently uses in order to keep track?
Training	How to handle disgruntled or aggressive patrons who are used to the previous service How to handle people claiming to be retirees, etc., who cannot afford to pay
Work flows	How logically and sensitively to stop discussions after five minutes in order to explain the new system How to move from the free discussion to setting the 'meter'

Performance

What happens if the information he gives out, at $50 an hour, is incorrect? Is there legal liability?

What sort of performance measures are kept?—Is he expected to earn money for the department?

EXERCISE 7.2

The steps involved in moving the library would include

1. advising staff and students of library closure
2. ensuring that the new building has shelving, computer outlets, phones, etc. that work
3. organizing boxes and movers
4. packing books and other materials in order
5. maintaining records of what is packed where
6. moving boxes across to new building
7. unpacking in correct order
8. installing equipment
9. advising staff and students when reopened.

Your chart should look something like this:

Activity Week

	1	2	3	4	5	6	7	8
1.	*****							
2.		******						
3.		****						
4.		***************						
5.		**************						
6.		******************					
7.			************************				
8.				*****************		
9.					*******		

EXERCISE 8.1

Katrina will need to consider

Clear goals

Get three students to research the three environmental organizations and three to research oil industry, real estate development, and nuclear power industry policies.

Events and activities

Have teams present poster sessions on each of the above; stage a public debate on environmental policy with students representing both the environmental organizations' and the industries' perspectives.

Finance	Little expense is required.
Promotion	Get teachers involved; put materials in library; give handouts to students; promote attendance at poster sessions and debate.

EXERCISE 8.2

Adrian will need to deal with, among other things:

- determining what will the band charge—can we afford them?
- meeting and greeting the band
- looking after them when they've arrived—ensuring that catering, accommodation are suitable
- whether to have a post-concert party
- making sure enough power is available for speakers, instruments, etc.
- security and audience control
- ticketing and seating for guests
- ensuring the band gets away OK
- proper publicity
- backup plan if the band has to cancel at the last minute.

EXERCISE 9.1

Victoria will need to consider:

Legislation	Minimum space requirements, adequate lighting, ergonomic workstations, occupational safety and health
Discuss with team	How do they feel about the conditions? Problems, solutions?
Equipment	Is it adequate? Does she need an ergonomic specialist to evaluate the equipment?
Conditions	Discuss with union representatives

EXERCISE 9.2

Jan will have to consider:

Responsibility	What is the department's freedom of information policy? Who may agree to the request, authorize it to proceed, or deny it? Who undertakes the work? Who deals with requester?
Record keeping	Maintaining records of requests, authorizations for release, work involved, etc.
Nature of request	Categorizing requests for future analysis Sensitive material
Reporting	Providing details for annual reports Responding to congressional inquiries
Charging	Who decides? Who administers if there is a charge?

EXERCISE 10.1

Criteria Keiko might use include:

- Do applicants have at least one year's experience working in a library?
- Do they have experience in more than one area of a library?
- Do they have library technician qualifications?
- Is their written application neat, concise, and responsive to the selection criteria?
- Do they have recent references?
- Do they have additional special skills that may be useful, e.g., a second language?
- Do they live locally?

EXERCISE 10.2

The headings used and reasons for inclusion might include:

Attendance and punctuality
> An important part of any job; all employers concerned

Ability to work in a team
> Virtually all work will involve a team at some stage. It is important that everyone can work cooperatively.

Relations with management/supervision
> Having an appropriate way of dealing with management, responding to supervision

Accuracy and quality of work
> Highly important in any job

General attitude
> Need to show initiative and enthusiasm, and generally to be pleasant to work with

Verbal and written communication skills
> Necessary in any workplace

Computer aptitude
> Also relates to how quickly they can pick up a new task. Again, important in virtually all jobs.

EXERCISE 11.1

Marion might consider these strategies:

Clear purpose	With the team, write down the major goals and timeframes. Get the team to go through the goals and be sure everyone fully understands and is committed to them.
Clear roles and assignments	With the team, break the work into manageable pieces and assign responsibilities. Ensure everyone is clear on each other's roles and objectives. Do the tasks and role assignments match individual strengths?

External relations	Identify existing useful contacts of team members. Ask each team member to identify a new contact within their own organization, and one externally, who will be useful.
Consensus decisions	For all major decisions have full team participation. Ensure that objections and concerns are discussed in detail. Avoid tight deadlines as far as possible, to allow for adequate discussion.
Shared leadership	Build a sense of team responsibility for decisions. As team leader, take a low profile unless the team is having problems.
Listening	Practice active listening, making sure all concerns are properly dealt with. Try to pick up unvoiced concerns by watching body language, attitudes, comments, etc.

EXERCISE 11.2

Huong may try to take these steps:

Information	Engage in a brainstorming session to identify future growth. Encourage team to discuss work levels, compare with previous years.
Initiating	Have a team discussion regarding training and development needs. Investigate opportunities to broaden, modify the work flows.
Clarifying	Make sure team is clear on goals. Work with team to set standards.
Harmonizing	Study the interpersonal dynamics in the team. Is counseling necessary? Would opportunities for staff rotation help?
Encouraging	Build a highly positive climate by being very supportive. Genuinely seek new ideas. Consider how appropriate behavior may be rewarded.
Coordinating and controlling	In consultation with staff, set agreed targets for relatively short periods. Appoint team leaders responsible for achieving targets. Get team to assess resource requirements necessary to meet targets.

EXERCISE 12.1

The costs involved would include:

Fixed	Purchase of the van and its depreciation over a number of years Additional book stock Circulation system in the van

Equipment such as photocopier or computers installed in the van
Staffing (usually fixed but could be variable if patronage increased sufficiently to require another staff member)

Variable   Diesel and related running costs
Maintenance
Cost of consumables

Long-term   Replacing van
Demand for extension of service
Impact on existing branches

EXERCISE 12.2

The costs to consider include:

Research   Employment of a research assistant or use of existing staff
Accessing online resources, printing and photocopying
Visits to various libraries, agencies
Expert to check text
Copyright clearance on graphics

Production   Graphics
Layout, word processing, editing, photocopying, photography, etc.
Binding and collating

Marketing   Advertising and promotion
Postage, packaging, transport, etc.
Charging?
Distribution on request to individuals, organizations other than schools?

EXERCISE 13.1

The groups will probably have the following needs:

Administration   Inquiries about anniversaries, current and past issues, materials for PR campaigns, material on prominent alumni, etc.
(Should be given high priority—they fund the archives!)

Faculty   May want material on the development of courses, previous staff members, history of their departments, etc.

Grad students   Material on courses, university history, notable staff/students

Undergrads   Research projects for history classes, majors

Local media   Anniversaries, etc.—a university is an important local institution

National media   Anniversaries, deaths, controversies, grants, research background

The public   Questions about their student days, photographs of individuals, sports teams, etc.

EXERCISE 13.2

Ali will be concerned with:

Customers	Broadly, commercial (TV, radio, press) and individual (the public) Also serious researchers, related institutions, politicians, etc.—how will each group be treated?
Priorities	How are priorities set? Does paying for service affect priorities? What if you don't live in the city? Is a TV station with a deadline more important than an individual on vacation with only a few hours in the city?
Service levels	How much time is spent on one inquiry? Does it matter whether you pay? Does it matter whether you are local or out of town? Does it matter whether the subject is easy to deal with or more demanding?
Cost/benefit	What does the museum gain from its research center? Can it afford to run it free? Should people pay?
Staffing	Should staff specialize in areas or be generalists? Do they all work at the desk or do some deal only with telephone, email or written enquiries?

EXERCISE 14.1

José might use the following variables:

Staff level	He could target senior management, middle management, all new employees, etc.
Areas of specialization	Legal, marketing, research, human resources, etc.
Location	All staff in the main office, those in the warehouse, those in the field, etc.
Staff groups	Those doing further study, those involved on a specific project, etc.

EXERCISE 14.2

Maria might promote her activity by:
- visiting local preschools and talking with staff
- leaving flyers at local preschools for parents to pick up when collecting children
- placing posters in preschools, shopping centers, etc.
- making sure promotion inside the library is clear and visible
- providing sessions at different times on various days in different branches
- contacting local shop owners, service organizations, businesses, etc., to try to get sponsorship in order to enable bigger, bolder events to be held
- using fancy dress or rented costumes to promote particular themes.

EXERCISE 15.2

Carmel and her staff may be concerned with the following questions:

Location, transportation
- Will the new site be near public transportation?
- Will it have adequate parking—free or charged?
- Is it generally easy for staff to reach?
- Is it near stores, banks, restaurants, etc.?
- Is the neighborhood safe?

Formal/informal relations
- How will staff who have moved keep in contact with their colleagues?
- What about meetings involving both groups?
- Will the relocated staff be 'out of sight, out of mind'?
- If senior management is still in the old building, will it maintain an appropriate level of contact?

Facilities
- Are facilities in the new building as good as before, e.g., toilets, break room, cafeteria?
- Is the office accommodation at an appropriate standard?
- Will people still have offices, or as much space?

Working conditions
- Are conditions in the new place as good?
- Is it air conditioned, light, and pleasant to work in?

Access to resources
- Will the computer system be networked to the new building?
- How about mail delivery?
- Access to the library, etc., if they are still in the old building?

Self-image, status
- Staff may be working in a boring office building instead of a historic, heritage building—how will that affect them?
- Will staff feel committed to the organization when away from its headquarters?

EXERCISE 16.1

Jean might propose the following changes:

Environment
- Automatic opening doors
- Improved lighting
- Improved floor coverings
- Better desks; physical arrangements to enable the public, particularly the elderly, to be dealt with in a comfortable setting
- Creation of one or two offices to deal with more private inquiries

Systems
- Better signage outside and inside
- Self-service facilities inside that may reduce face-to-face questions
- Prominently displayed handouts on the most frequently asked questions
- Computers at the desk to enable instant access to city records

| Differences | Designing a way, perhaps via elevator or through another entrance, to allow the elderly or disabled easy access to the building |
| | Having a desk and seating area big enough to cope with large maps or plans |

EXERCISE 16.2

As the manager you could:

- review the service contract on the building, with a view to more regular inspections
- consider employing a security company to check the building outside working hours
- obtain quotes and recommendations from builders to install a better drainage system
- ensure that you or a member of staff inspect the building every day or two, particularly if heavy rain is forecast

If emergency procedures are not already in place, have them developed and make sure that staff know what to do at the first signs of trouble.

EXERCISE 17.2

While there are rarely clear-cut solutions in these situations, the following points should be considered:

1. If you alert management about the value of the LP, how will they sell it? Is it ethical for you to offer $100 for it? Is it worth getting an independent valuation? If you asked management whether you could take a couple of LPs home without telling them the value and they agreed, would it be OK?

2. Is this change fair to the paid employees or the volunteers? What could you say to management, union representatives? Could alternatives be offered to the displaced employees?

3. There is a problem with your accepting this 'free' subscription—can it be seen as a bribe? Might it make you obligated to the representative? Might you suggest that the library get the benefit of the representative's generosity?—i.e., that the magazine should come to the library, rather than to you personally?

4. Your becoming Linda's supervisor could be seen as favoritism, even though you did not recommend the move. Both you and Linda may find it awkward. Instead you might invite everyone on the staff to apply, and select the best qualified from among them.

GLOSSARY

This glossary contains the main terms used in this book. For a comprehensive glossary, see Farkas, Lynn, *LibrarySpeak: a glossary of terms in librarianship and information management.*

access to information *See* freedom of information

accountability Taking responsibility for an action

accounting period The timeframe for reporting on financial transactions. Generally, this is a period of one year (e.g., July through June), but it may vary

active listening Concentrating on what the other person is saying in order to understand fully what they mean, avoiding your own interpretation

antidiscrimination Promoting a climate where all staff are treated fairly regardless of particular characteristics such as gender, ethnicity, sexual preference, etc.

assessment Evaluating the progress of an individual or a work program against a set of criteria

ATI *See* freedom of information

auditability Having systems, particularly financial ones, that enable another person to follow exactly what was done in the past

budget A financial plan based upon the estimated expenditure related to a project, process, etc.

budget cycle Similar to the accounting period, it is the timeframe in which money allocated should be spent—e.g., money allocated for salaries in 2003 must be spent during that year

budget-neutral Covering the cost of a program, etc. through the revenue it raises

change advocate A key staff member who is won over to the new procedure and subsequently advocates its implementation on a wider scale

change agent A person who is a key figure in promoting and implementing the change process

code of ethics A written code outlining an organization's ethical principles and rules of staff conduct

commitment An undertaking or promise given to perform a particular task or duty

conceptual skills Skills dealing with broad philosophical issues that shape an organization's direction in the longer term

consensus Acceptance of a decision by all parties

constraint A difficulty or limitation that affects the manner in which a task can be done

copyright The intellectual property that resides in any published or unpublished work

corporate governance The system of rules, policies and processes by which an organization is run, including legislative requirements and internal regulations

corporate responsibility The commitment by an organization to manage its activities in an ethical way that contributes to the society in which it operates

critical path analysis A method for determining the most time-consuming stages of a project. *See also* PERT network

cross-training *Also* multi-skilling. Broadening the range of skills of individuals through training and development activities

curriculum vitae CV. An outline of an individual's education and employment history, usually attached to job applications

customer satisfaction pyramid The levels of service from basic to excellent that customers receive. Organizations aim to move their service level to the top of the pyramid

customer service policy Usually a written policy detailing how customers will be treated and their questions dealt with

CV *See* curriculum vitae

cycle of appropriation Essentially the budget cycle—when money is received and the date by which it has to be expended

disaster management plan A written document providing a series of steps to take in the event of an emergency

discretionary funding That part of the budget that lower-level management control directly

duty of care A legal term denoting the responsibility that an individual has in maintaining a safe environment for staff and users

EEO *See* equal employment opportunity

encumbrance An order placed but not yet paid for

equal employment opportunity EEO. State and federal legislation aimed at eliminating discrimination in the workplace based on sex, marital status, race, etc.

ethos The philosophy or general approach that is an integral part of an organization and its character

evaluation Assessing an individual or a program against an agreed set of criteria

external environment The 'world' outside the control of an organization

feasibility A test commonly undertaken to assess whether or not a course of action is likely to succeed as expected

feedback Response from staff or users to an action. In virtually all situations, feedback is an important element and should be encouraged

fee for service A philosophy arguing that users should pay the direct cost of the service they wish to use

fixed cost A cost associated with running a program that cannot easily be changed in the short term

FOI *See* freedom of information

formal internal environment The environment within an organization that is promoted by management through procedures, philosophy, etc.

freedom of information A citizen's right to access information held by their government

front-line manager A lower-level manager or supervisor who does not oversee the work of other managers

functional design Organizational design that groups work by function, i.e., what is actually being done

Gantt chart A bar chart showing when each task of a project should start and end

human resource management All aspects of personnel management within an organization

implementation Putting a new practice or procedure into operation

incremental budgeting Using a previous year's figure as a base and adding or subtracting a percentage from this figure in order to arrive at the new amount. *See also* program-based budgeting, zero-based budgeting

induction program *See* orientation program

input Making comments and suggestions and providing advice to any decision-making process

internal environment The environment inside an organization comprising the formal (prescribed by management) and the informal (developed by staff and individuals)

job description A written description of what main tasks are expected in a job

learning organization An organization that encourages staff to continuously develop their skills and modify their ideas in order to easily transform and adapt to rapid change

management The process of planning, organizing, leading, and controlling in order to get things done effectively with and through others

Margerison-McCann Team Management Systems Development International TMSDI. A commercially available analysis tool aimed at assessing how an individual works with others

market segment *Also* target group. A group of customers or patrons who share common needs or interests. Services can be designed and products targeted differently for different market segments

MBTI *See* Myers-Briggs Type Indicator

mechanistic design A traditional organizational design based on clearly defined lines such as function, product, geography, etc.

mentoring Sponsoring and supporting another, often lower-level, staff member

middle manager A person who directs the activities of other staff, including front-line managers

mission statement *Also* vision statement. A short statement outlining the purpose of an organization

modeling Using a physical or computer model to simulate real-life situations for testing purposes

multi-skilling *See* cross-training

Myers-Briggs Type Indicator MBTI. A commercially available analysis tool aimed at identifying individual differences in approaching decision-making

nondiscretionary funding Money over which lower-level management have no immediate control

occupational safety and health OSH. *Also* occupational health and safety, OHS. Legal requirements for ensuring a safe workplace

OHS *See* occupational safety and health

operational planning *Also* tactical planning. Planning concerned primarily with short-term activities that relate to overall objectives

organic design An organizational structure that is flexible according to the work or project being undertaken at a particular time

organizational culture The same as the internal environment, comprising both formal and informal cultures

organizational structure *Also* structure. The way an organization is broken down into sections or divisions

orientation program *Also* induction program. A formal program used to inform and assist new employees in the workplace

OSH *See* occupational safety and health

output A measurable quantity of product or service achieved from given inputs

performance appraisal The process of evaluating staff work performance against previously agreed goals

performance measure A means of assessing performance that may be qualitative or quantitative

PERT network Program Evaluation and Review Technique. A network chart that shows the steps needed to complete a task, the sequence in which they must be undertaken, and the time they will take to complete

pilot study A small-scale test to study the effectiveness of a planned project

privacy The natural right to keep information about one's life private and not readily available to anyone

probationary period Usually three or six months, it is a testing period in which management can decide whether new staff are acceptable as permanent staff members

product design The manner in which all aspects of a product are shaped in order to meet its goals

program-based budgeting An approach to financial budgeting based upon the cost of achieving a particular objective. *See also* incremental budgeting, zero-based budgeting

Program Evaluation and Review Technique *See* PERT network

project group *See* task force

qualitative measure A measure that is to some degree subjective and based upon an individual's perception of quality or correctness—e.g., whether a reference question is thought to have been answered well may depend to some degree on the knowledge of the client

quantitative measure An assessment measure based on numbers—e.g., the number of books circulated in a day

resources All the material things necessary to achieve a goal—i.e., people, money, and things

simulation Similar to modeling, simulation uses a model to test real-world activities on a smaller scale

span of control The number of staff for which a manager is responsible

strategic objective A major, long-term objective important to the survival of the organization

strategic planning Planning dealing with long-term, strategic objectives and how to achieve them

structure *See* organizational structure

supervisor A front-line manager dealing with the day-to-day running of an area

SWOT Strengths, weaknesses, opportunities, threats. A way of assessing the internal and external environments of an organization

tactical planning *See* operational planning

target group *See* market segment

task force *Also* project group. Staff from various areas gathered together to work on a specific project or task

team A work group comprising several individuals working toward the same goals

team building A method of developing dynamic, achieving teams. Useful when a team seems to be underperforming

timeframe The time period in which a task is to be started and completed

time management Techniques aimed at helping people use time more effectively

TMSDI *See* Margerison-McCann Team Management Systems Development International

top management Senior management concerned primarily with the long-term strategy of an organization

unreasonable request A request that appears, given the resources and priorities of an area, to be impossible to complete in the time allowed

variable cost A cost associated with an activity that changes directly according to the amount of that activity undertaken

vision statement *See* mission statement

zero-based budgeting A financial budgeting system which assumes that all activities start from scratch at the beginning of each period and have to be costed out as such. *See also* incremental budgeting, program-based budgeting

INDEX

LEARN LIBRARY SKILLS SERIES

This series of paperback workbooks introduces skills needed by library science students and library technicians, as well as librarians seeking refresher materials or study guides for in-service training classes. Each book teaches essential professional skills in a step-by-step process, accompanied by numerous practical examples, exercises and quizzes to reinforce learning, and an appropriate glossary.

Learn About Information
International Edition ©2015
Helen Rowe
ISBN: 9781590954331 Paperback

Learn Basic Library Skills
International Edition ©2015
Helen Rowe and Trina Grover
ISBN: 9781590954348 Paperback

Learn Cataloging the RDA Way
International Edition ©2015
Lynn Farkas and Helen Rowe
ISBN: 9781590954355 Paperback

Learn Dewey Decimal Classification (Edition 23)
International Edition ©2015
Lynn Farkas
ISBN: 9781590954362 Paperback

Learn Library Management
International Edition ©2015
Jacinta Ganendran
ISBN: 9781590954379 Paperback

Learn Library of Congress Classification
International Edition ©2015
ISBN: 9781590954386 Paperback

Learn Library of Congress Subject Access
International Edition ©2015
Lynn Farkas
ISBN 9781590954393 Paperback

Learn Reference Work
International Edition ©2015
ISBN: 9781590954416 Paperback

LIBRARY SCIENCE TITLES

LibrarySpeak:
A Glossary of Terms in Librarianship and Information Technology,
International Edition ©2015
Lynn Farkas
ISBN: 9781590954423 Paperback

My Mentoring Diary:
A Resource for the Library and Information Professions
Revised Edition ©2015
Ann Ritchie and Paul Genoni
ISBN: 9781590954430 Paperback

Quality in Library Service:
A Competency-Based Staff Training Program
International Edition ©2015
Jennifer Burrell and Brad McGrath
ISBN: 9781590954447 Paperback

TOTALRECALL PUBLICATIONS, INC.
1103 Middlecreek,
Friendswood, TX 77546-5448

Phone: (281) 992-3131
email: Sales@TotalRecallPress.com
Online: www.totalrecallpress.com

CPSIA information can be obtained
at www.ICGtesting.com
Printed in the USA
LVHW100725040821
694459LV00002B/3